It's Time to Remember, AMERICA!

CONNECTING THE PAST WITH THE PRESENT

MICHAEL R. MYERS

HORIZON BOOKS

A DIVISION OF CHRISTIAN PUBLICATIONS, INC.
CAMP HILL, PENNSYLVANIA

Horizon Books
a division of Christian Publications, Inc.
3825 Hartzdale Drive
Camp Hill, PA 17011
www.cpi-horizon.com

ISBN: 0-88965-149-3

Contents

Foreword

Americans are so ignorant of their past that they have become "prisoners of the present," according to Pulitzer Prize-winning historian Daniel J. Boorstin. "Obsessed with where we are, we have forgotten where we came from and how we got here." Boorstin concludes that, as a result, we are finding it ever harder to "keep our bearings in the streams of history."

Michael Myers' *It's Time to Remember, America!* not only can help us regain our historical bearings, but it could also have several profoundly positive consequences. Through its abundant use of original documents and primary sources, it could open even skeptical eyes to see that this country has authentic spiritual and moral roots.

For many others, especially parents and teachers, the organized documentation of *It's Time to Remember, America!* could help them respond to one of this nation's most serious and far-reaching problems: the gross failure of American education.

This splendid book is based in part on research from author Michael Myers' own teaching at the fine school he established and directs, Dayspring Christian Academy in Lancaster, Pennsylvania. It will help reverse this troubling trend in our schools. It will be valuable not only for its author's uniquely clear insights and its array of pertinent quotations verifying specific aspects of America's Christian history, but for its highly constructive citations of related volumes and educational institutions, especially the pioneering work of Verna M. Hall and Rosalie J. Slater, cofounders of the Foundation for American Christian Education.

Mike Myers is right. It's time to remember, America—time to remember our godly history, our Christian example to the nations, the consequences of passions gone astray, the value of our national identity and of the biblical principles on which we were built!

Charles Hull Wolfe
President, Restore the Republic

Introduction

Something of great consequence is stirring across America today. It is not confined to any one segment of society or to a particular geographical area. Young and old alike are experiencing a yearning, a longing to know the truth about our roots—our national beginnings.

In the wake of the multicultural tidal wave that has swept through our political institutions and schools in recent years, Americans are beginning to search for the meaning of America. Healthy questions are being asked about the foundations of this great nation: "Was there a central, noble purpose behind the establishment of the United Sates of America or, rather, did our individuality as a nation simply evolve out of the enlightened thought of that age? Was it simply a natural progression toward the full attainment of human rights?"

On the surface, using modern sources, one may find ready answers and opinions to these questions. Certainly, current textbooks and histories are rife with politically correct rationales and scenarios explaining the founding of America. This superficial treatment of America's story has produced both apathy and listlessness among the populace. With no anchor to the past, no mooring to the secure bedrock of antiquity, there is little to give genuine meaning to our present existence.

What would happen if we were able to return to the colonial and founding eras, or even go back a hundred years? If we could speak with the men and women who influenced the tides of change during our formative years, what stories would they tell? Would their accounts align squarely with today's filtered version?

While we cannot travel back to an earlier time, we can take advantage of the voluminous writings of that age. Preserved for posterity are the thoughts, aspirations, beliefs and hopes of the great leaders of yesteryear. With painstaking diligence, these statesmen and scholars recorded events and perceptions in journals and notebooks. They made eloquent speeches and wrote copious letters. Thus, we have a veritable feast of rich documentation from which to partake in answering the questions about our genesis. Much can be learned from examining the view and perceptions of these people who had personally experienced the rising of the American star.

The purpose of this book is twofold. It is an attempt, through the use of original documents and primary sources, to canvass and rehearse the voices of our American ancestors—those who have gone before, laying down their lives as stepping-stones for us who have come later. The object is to glean the wisdom of the ages on certain topics or subjects of significance.

Few would dispute the fact that the men and women who shaped this nation were a rare breed of individuals who overcame insurmountable odds to establish a system of government like nothing the world had ever known. With multiple forces pulling on the fabric of American order from all sides, it behooves us to pause and reflect on what the great ones of our past believed. Their insight and sagacity, proven over time, offer hope and inspiration to a generation deficient in both.

The second purpose of the book is to verify that America had a unique beginning with a distinctively Christian purpose. As we read and reflect upon the views of our founders and subsequent American leaders, we can readily identify a biblical worldview. As we read the many speeches, narratives, personal messages and diaries from the people who lived during the first 300 years of our history, we find a common thread of belief. Indeed, this thread is more like a strong cord to which all the intentions, determinations and decisions of the primary players of our history are fastened.

There can be no doubt that the prevailing worldview of the colonial and founding periods of this nation was a biblical Christian one. Its imprint is everywhere noticed. Even from the most profane and secular voices came the essential absolutes of right and wrong. Decisions and documents reflected the Truth as proclaimed in the Bible. The kindly influence of Christianity infiltrated and tempered all that the early Americans touched. True, for some this was almost an involuntary reaction over which they had little control. For the majority, however, adherence to the biblical creed was by design and deliberate intention.

It was not the idealism of the Greek philosophers that gave rise to the inspired view of the essential equality of man; it was the doctrine of the Bible that proclaimed that man was created in the image of God. This Christian idea liberated all who would embrace its teaching—eventually freeing even those who were still in bondage at our inception. Likewise, it was not the grandeur of the Roman system of law that gave rise to our American republican form of government. It was the Hebrew republic, with its reliance upon the Law of God and the principle of representation, that provided the greater precedent.

That America was established by God for His eternal purposes was an idea that was unashamedly spoken by such men as George Washington, John Adams, Patrick Henry and Abraham Lincoln to name a few. It was this belief, emblazoned upon the hearts of individuals, that provided the courage and determination for the Pilgrims to "reform without tarrying for any" and men like Nathan Hale to proclaim, "I only regret that I have but one life to give for my country."

Those who lived through the miraculous adventure of our national birth held a remarkably consistent biblical worldview. Would it not be prudent for us, today, to likewise embrace their discernment? Is it not incumbent upon us to pass this revered and accepted purpose for America on to the generations coming behind us? Nearly universal is the desire of all parents to pass their beliefs and attitudes about life and existence, intact, to their children. Great pains are generally taken to ensure that family histories, traditions and views are inculcated into the young.

Sadly, on a national scale, this time-honored custom has failed. Slowly, insidiously, the truths and values upon which America was founded have been extracted from our national memory. The very ideals and beliefs that gave impetus to the rise of our republic have become passé, out of vogue, even ridiculed and openly scorned. How could this have happened? As Thomas Jefferson once said, "The price of freedom is eternal vigilance." So it was that as American Christians and the Church settled into security and prosperity, the tendrils of secularism, humanism and finally, neo-paganism have quietly fastened themselves upon our institutions, our churches and our children.

Is America without hope? Have we lost the golden era forever? Will this nation continue to evolve into something quite contrary to what her original design intended?

The answers to these questions lie primarily within the hearts of this generation. We have reached a great divide in the road. The paths diverge in opposite directions. One leads to fragmentation, division, disease, loss of freedom and individuality. The other proceeds to order, harmony, unity and peace.

I believe the very future of America will be decided by this generation. With so great a cloud of witnesses who have gone before us, how will we cast our lot? Will we stand up for righteousness, exalt virtuous living and proclaim the Truth to a lost and dying world? I believe that we have the character and resolve to "rebuild the ancient ruins; . . . raise up the age-old foundations; . . . be called the repairer of the breach, the restorer of the streets in which to dwell" (Isaiah 58:12). We have lost our way. We have forgotten our past. We are not without hope, however, for we still have access to the truth of our past and to God's Word that never fails. Therefore, let us remove the cobwebs from our national memory and shine forth the light of God's Hand in our history. May this book enlighten your heart and inspire you to action.

It's time to remember, America!

★   ★   ★

On America
and Patriotism

Pa′triotism, n. Love of one's country;
the passion which aims to serve one's
country, either in defending it from in-
vasion or protecting its rights and
maintaining its laws and institutions in
vigor and purity. Patriotism is the char-
acteristic of a good citizen, the noblest
passion that animates a man in the
character of a citizen.[1]

*If I forget thee, O Jerusalem, let my right
hand forget her cunning. If I do not remember thee, let my tongue cleave to the roof of
my mouth; if I prefer not Jerusalem above
my chief joy. (Psalm 137:5-6, KJV)*

*Blessed is the nation whose God is the
LORD, the people whom He has chosen for
His own inheritance. (Psalm 33:12)*

*Righteousness exalts a nation, but sin is a
disgrace to any people. (Proverbs 14:34)*

America! Just the name has evoked deep emotion and highest aspirations for personal liberty and fulfillment in countless millions in the short while that this nation has existed as the "land of the free and the home of the brave." For those who call this country their own, a deep pride swells up as they reflect upon the majesty and powerful influence of America. Many who have left these shores realize the special blessings and privileges of America. The liberty and prosperity of the United States become eminently clear and longed for by an American away from home.

Yet another America has emerged with increasing intensity—an America without morals, an America without virtue, an America without Christian values. We are hateful and jealous. We are lost in many ways.

Our response to this duality will determine the final outcome of the present struggle. Will God abandon America? What can and will American Christians do to salvage our faltering culture? The answer, I believe, lies in the veracity with which we claim our Christian heritage, using ancient landmarks to steer the course for future generations. In order to save America, we must understand and appreciate America's past.

Historically, patriotism has been a much appreciated character trait. And yet today there are many who would shy away from its call. Scripture teaches us that God establishes nations as His way of structuring human civilization on earth (Genesis 10; Jeremiah 18).

While we must take care never to exalt any nation above God and His eternal purposes, it seems wise and proper to embrace one's country with a love which would spur it on to excellence in the calling God has for it. Without patriotism, we tend to lose sight of God's plan and purpose for our nation. What follows is a seemingly pious, but misguided separation of Christian influence from human society and government. Apathy and complacency turn into outright disgust and despair. Clearly this is not the way to restoration and revival!

As American Christians, our hearts should break for our nation, even as Jesus wept over His (Luke 19:41). We should influence our culture for righteousness, even as Jesus was actively involved in reforming the atrocities of His day (19:45). Following Christ's example, let us respond to His commission to spread salt and light into the land in which God has planted us. This begins with the individual ordering his life according to the principles and precepts for godly living laid out in Scripture.

It then moves outward to the spheres of the family, the church and finally to the neighborhood and beyond. Christ's Law of Love must govern our relationships in all of these spheres. Furthermore, as American Christians, we must prepare leaders to assume positions of responsibility and influence in every area of life.

God has granted us remarkable liberty in this nation. May our love for our country grow ever stronger as we remember her miraculous origins. May

Following Christ's example, let us lift our sights and spread salt and light into the land in which God has planted us.

this love compel us to seek to correct the wrong things in our nation; to restore her to the biblical standard of morality and justice. May God pour out His mercy and grace on our land.

★   ★   ★

". . . it is not our own arm which has saved us"

One can recognize the almost palpable pride of Samuel Adams in this speech. Adams does not, however, lose sight of the greater Being at work in America's rise to grandeur.

> We are now on this continent . . . three millions of souls united in one common cause. We have large armies. . . . Foreign nations are waiting to crown our success by their alliances. There are instances of, I would say, an almost astonishing Providence in our favor; our success has staggered our enemies, and almost given faith to infidels; so that we may truly say it is not our own arm which has saved us.
>
> The hand of heaven appears to have led us on to be, perhaps, humble instruments and means in the great providential dispensation which is completing.[2]

Patriotism and humility before God are necessary ingredients for a national spiritual revival!

*It's time to remember
our humble beginnings!*

"Give me your tired, your poor . . ."

Our forefathers saw America as a "city set upon a hill"—a beacon to all the nations of the world declaring the blessings of a nation whose God is the Lord (Psalm 33:12). This could be termed America's gospel purpose. Samuel Adams saw the United States as a haven for the oppressed and abused of the world.

> . . . freedom of thought and the right of private judgment, in matters of conscience, driven from every corner of the earth, direct their course to this happy country as their last asylum. Let us cherish the noble guests, and shelter them under the wings of an universal toleration. Be this the seat of unbounded religious freedom.[3]

The spirit of his message is embodied in the Statue of Liberty's motto: "Give me your tired, your poor, your huddled masses yearning to breathe free . . ." Let us embrace the downtrodden and needy and lead them to the Light of the World who offers hope to all who come.

It's time to remember our gospel purpose!

". . . to owe to his hand and power . . ."

Long before the American War for Independence, God was planting the seeds of this Christian republic in the various colonies. His handprint is firmly pressed into the soil of each unique genesis. William Penn, Quaker preacher and proprietor of the Pennsylvania colony, realized the providence of God in its foundation:

> For my country, I eyed the Lord in obtaining it, and more was I drawn to look to him, and to owe to his hand and power than to any other way. I have so obtained it, and desire to keep it that I may not be unworthy of his love. . . .[4]

May we embrace these same sentiments as we dedicate our lives to securing the blessings of our Heavenly Father for our beloved land!

It's time to remember the hand of God in our nation's history!

". . . *its ornament and safeguard*"

John Hancock, first to sign the Declaration of Independence and thereby lay his very life on the line, had a distinct vision of what made America great.

> But I thank God, that America abounds in men who are superior to all temptation, whom nothing can divert from a steady pursuit of the interest of their country; who are at once its ornament and safeguard. And sure as I am, I should not incur your displeasure, if I paid a respect, so justly due to their much honored characters, in this place. . . . From them let us, my friends, take example; from them let us catch the divine enthusiasm. . . .[5]

Hancock saw the people of America as its strength. Tragically, the Christian testimony and example of many of the heroes of our past have been forgotten or systematically removed from our histories. We must proclaim the stories of the people who shaped this nation in our homes and classrooms. Through diligent research we can discover anew the wisdom and contribution of men like those examined in this book. That same ennobled and enlightened character seen in the patriots of old can be restored and help guide us through the challenges of our modern world.

It's time to remember our heroes!

". . . to sacrifice . . . to the sacred calls of his country"

Countless men and women of our founding era gave unselfishly of their possessions and lives so that we may enjoy the blessings of liberty. James Otis, perhaps the preeminent New England orator at the time of the Revolution, spoke of the cost of patriotism.

> The only principles of public conduct, that are worthy of a gentleman or a man, are to sacrifice estate, ease, health and applause, and even life, to the sacred calls of his country.
>
> These manly sentiments, in private life, make the good citizens; in public life, the patriot and the hero.[6]

Have we attained that degree of commitment to the purposes of God for our nation in order to restore and preserve our liberty so dearly bought?

It's time to remember the price of our freedom!

". . . a humble anticipation of the future blessings . . ."

First president George Washington had an early and acute appreciation for the nature of the fledgling nation that was taking root. America was like no other nation in its founding and principles of government.

> No people can be bound to acknowledge and adore the invisible hand, which conducts the affairs of men, more than the people of the United States. Every step, by which they have advanced to the character of an independent nation, seems to have been distinguished by some token of providential agency; and . . . cannot be compared with the means by which most governments have been established, without some return of pious gratitude along with a humble anticipation of the future blessings which the past seems to presage.[7]

Washington showed fatherly concern for the nation in the years of growth ahead. America must guard against sin.

> . . . we ought to be no less persuaded,
> that the propitious smiles of heaven
> can never be expected on a nation that
> disregards the eternal rules of order
> and right, which heaven itself has or-
> dained. . . .[8]

Washington saw America as having a mission to the nations of the world. Through her
example, others would find the truth of Christian liberty—both spiritual and civil.

> I . . . [wish] that heaven may continue to
> give you the choicest tokens of its be-
> neficence; that your union and brotherly
> affection may be perpetual; that the free
> constitution, which is the work of your
> hands, may be sacredly maintained; that
> its administration, in every department,
> be stamped with wisdom and virtue;
> that, in fine the happiness of the people
> of these States, under the auspices of lib-
> erty, may be made complete by so care-
> ful a preservation and so prudent a use
> of this blessing as will acquire to them
> the glory of recommending it to the ap-
> plause, the affection, and adoption of
> every nation which is yet a stranger to
> it.[9]

*It's time to remember
our Christian example to the nations!*

"... cultivate peace and harmony with all ..."

The wisdom and farsightedness of our first president can be seen as he expounded on the impact of righteous living and righteous government on America and the world.

> Observe good faith and justice towards all nations; cultivate peace and harmony with all; religion and morality enjoin this conduct; and can it be that good policy does not equally enjoin it? It will be worthy of a free, enlightened, and, at no distant period, a great nation, to give to mankind the magnanimous and too novel example of a people always guided by an exalted justice and benevolence.[10]

What a marvelous approach to foreign policy. Decisions would be based upon principles of right and justice, not on personal aggrandizement, sordid gain or positioning for power.

It's time to remember just dealings with others!

". . . control the usual current of passions . . . "

In the closing remarks of his farewell address, the beloved "Father of Our Country" warned of the excesses which destroy nations.

> In offering to you, my countrymen, these counsels of an old and affectionate friend, I dare not hope they will control the usual current of passions, or prevent our nation from running the course which has hitherto marked the destiny of nations . . . that they may now and then recur to moderate the fury of party spirit; to warn against mischiefs of foreign intrigues; to guard against the impostures of pretended patriotism. . . .[11]

There are those who, in the name of patriotism, may take America down a path that is contrary to the biblical standards of morality and justice. We must be ever vigilant against such potential harm.

It's time to remember the consequences of passions gone awry!

"America must be . . . independent in literature . . ."

Noah Webster, called "the nation's schoolmaster," played a tremendous role in forging the American people into a cohesive nation with a common identity. He labored tirelessly in this cause, focusing much of his effort in the area of education.

> However detestable personal pride may be, yet there is a national pride and a provincial, that are the noblest passions of the republican patriot. . . . For my own part, I frankly acknowledge, I have too much pride not to wish to see America assume a national character. I have too much pride to stand indebted to Great Britain for books to learn [sic] our children the letters of the alphabet. . . . America must be as independent in literature *as she is in* politics, *as famous for* arts *as for* arms. . . .[12]

Sadly, America is not only known for its rich literature, inspiring music and affecting art. America is now a major exporter of pornography and other types of immoral entertainment. This is not what Noah Webster had in mind for our national identity. May we return to a standard of decency and morality for which we can hold our heads high.

It's time to remember the value of our national identity!

"Intoxicated with unbroken success . . ."

Another great president, Abraham Lincoln, faced one of the darkest hours in American history. He read the signs of the times correctly when he recognized the need for America to come to grips with its sins against God and against one another. In his memorable proclamation setting aside Thursday, April 30, 1863 as a "Day of National Humiliation," Lincoln instructs the nation:

> We have been the recipients of the choicest bounties of heaven; we have been preserved these many years in peace and prosperity; we have grown in number, wealth, and power as no other Nation has ever grown. But we have forgotten God. We have forgotten the gracious hand which preserved us in peace and multiplied and enriched and strengthened us, and we have vainly imagined, in the deceitfulness of our hearts, that all the blessing were produced by some superior wisdom and virtue of our own. Intoxicated with unbroken success we have become too

self-sufficient to feel the necessity of re-
deeming and preserving grace, too
proud to pray to the God who made
us.

It behooves us then to humble ourselves before the offended Power, to
confess our national sins and to pray
for clemency and forgiveness.[13]

Sadly, this sobering assessment of our national spiritual condition is as true today as it
was in 1863.

It's time to remember to pray for forgiveness!

"... there is a God, and ... He hates injustice and slavery"

The issue of slavery touches the very heart of the meaning of liberty. Most certainly, many of the founders and early leaders of America grappled with this issue. For some, it was an anathema opposed to everything for which America stood. Others had a huge blind spot in this area. Jesus said in the Gospel of Matthew, "But if your eye is bad, your whole body will be full of darkness. If therefore the light that is in you is darkness, how great is the darkness!" (Matthew 6:23). President Lincoln addressed this very point:

> I know there is a God, and that He hates injustice and slavery. . . . Doesn't it appear strange that men can ignore the moral aspects of this contest? A revelation could not make it plainer to me that slavery or the Government must be destroyed. . . . It seems to me as if God had borne this thing, slavery, until the very teachers of religion have come to defend it from their Bible and to claim for it a divine character and sanction, and now the cup of iniquity is

full and the vial of wrath will be poured out.[14]

While the issue of slavery is no longer one of public debate, the same principles are involved in the intense controversies concerning homosexuality and abortion. These social questions are of the highest moral consideration, and they have the potential to divide and destroy our nation as nothing has since the slavery issue. We must be careful that we do not abrogate the Word of God in order to justify perversion and aberrance.

It's time to remember the uncompromising nature of God's Word!

". . . *patriotism is one of earth's highest virtues* . . ."

Over the years patriotism has gone in and out of vogue. For some, it is an intense and zealous passion that motivates extreme actions. For others it is almost an abomination which represents worldliness. John Ireland, former Archbishop of Saint Paul, Minnesota, extolled the virtues of patriotism from a biblical perspective.

> Pagan nations were wrong when they made gods of their noblest patriots. But the error was the excess of a great truth, that heaven unites with earth in approving and blessing patriotism; that patriotism is one of earth's highest virtues, worthy to have come down from the atmosphere of the skies.[15]

Let us not shrink from a pure love and concern for our nation because of the excesses of those who have taken patriotism to an extreme.

It's time to remember the validity of patriotism!

". . . the vital spark
of national honor . . ."

The value of patriotism to a people is above gold and precious stones, above commerce and industry, above citadels and warships. Patriotism is the vital spark of national honor; it is the fount of the nation's prosperity, the shield of the nation's safety. . . . Next to God is country, and next to religion is patriotism.[16]

So spoke Archbishop of St. Paul, Minnesota, John Ireland, in 1894. True patriotism springs from an appreciation for God's plan on earth. A nation's honor is ultimately tied to its relationship to God. If we truly love our nation, we will do all that we can to see that it remains in God's favor.

It's time to remember our nation's honor!

"The more thoroughly a nation deals with its history . . ."

Much of the miracle of America's birth and development has been deliberately excluded from textbooks for over 100 years. This fact has likely been a major contributor to the rise of secularism in our nation. The Reverend S.W. Foljambe made a profound observation in 1876:

> The more thoroughly a nation deals with its history, the more decidedly will it recognize and own an over-ruling Providence therein, and the more religious a nation it will become; while the more superficially it deals with its history, seeing only secondary causes and human agencies, the more irreligious it will be.[17]

If we want America to return to her greatness, we must restore her national memory by teaching the whole truth of our founding and purpose as a nation. We must restore the whole truth of our heritage to our nation's schools.

It's time to remember our godly history!

"We should never forget
. . . the prison . . ."

O ne of my favorite passages in Verna Hall's
The Christian History of the Constitution is an
excerpt from the preface to a 1700s history text
written by John Overton Choules:

> The glories of Christianity in England
> are to be traced in the sufferings of
> confessors and martyrs in the sixteenth
> and seventeenth centuries; and it was
> under the influence of Christian princi-
> ples, imbibed at this very period, that
> the *Mayflower* brought over the band of
> Pilgrims to Plymouth. . . . We should
> never forget that the prison, the scaf-
> fold, and the stake were stages in the
> march of civil and religious liberty
> which our forefathers had to travel, in
> order that we might attain our present
> liberty. . . . Before our children remove
> their religious connections . . . before
> they leave the old paths of God's Word
> . . . before they barter their birthright
> for a mess of pottage, let us place in
> their hands the chronicle of the glori-
> ous days of the suffering Churches,

and let them know that they are the
sons of the men "of whom the world
was not worthy," and whose suffering
for conscience' sake are here monu-
mentally recorded.[18]

Truly, the founding of America was a most
significant event. In a very real sense, it was the
flower from a divine planting, watered and
nurtured over the ages, purchased at a great
price. We must continue to tell the story; we
must not acquiesce to the omissions and falsi-
ties of those who would pervert and desecrate
the truth of our heritage.

It's time to remember
the cost of our liberty!

"Intelligence, patriotism, Christianity, and a firm reliance on Him . . ."

Lest we despair and lose hope for the restoration of America to her godly foundation, let us take heart from the words of Abraham Lincoln in his first inaugural address.

> Intelligence, patriotism, Christianity, and a firm reliance on Him who has never yet forsaken this favored land, are still competent to adjust in the best way all our present difficulty.[19]

Amazingly, we can still claim those words of Lincoln. God has not yet removed His hand of protection and blessing from our land. Difficult times have come and will certainly come again to help remind us of our dependence on Him who raised us up. Will God continue to shed His grace on America? Have we reached the end of the road as far as civilizations go? In this chapter we have examined both the glorious founding of our nation as well as the remedy for her ills. Let us take the message to heart and learn from our forefathers. Will America—can America—long endure, as Lincoln put it? The answer largely depends on people like you and me.

> If . . . My people who are called by My name humble themselves and pray, and seek My face and turn from their wicked ways, then I will hear from heaven, will forgive their sin, and will heal their land. (2 Chronicles 7:13-14)

It's time to remember our responsibility before God for our nation!

Long Live our Country! Oh, long through the undying ages may it stand, far removed in fact as in space from the Old World's feuds and follies, alone in its grandeur and its glory, itself the immortal monument of Him whom Providence commissioned to teach man the power of Truth, and to prove to the nations that their Redeemer liveth.[20]

Notes

[1] Noah Webster, *The American Dictionary of the English Language* (1828 facsimile edition, San Francisco: The Foundation for American Christian Education, 1967; 1995). Used by permission.

[2] Julian Hawthorne, ed., *Orations of American Orators* vol. I (New York: The Colonial Press, 1900), p. 9. "American Independence" by Samuel Adams. Delivered at the State House, Philadelphia, August 1, 1776.

[3] Ibid, p. 15.

[4] Verna M. Hall, *The Christian History of the Constitution of the United States of America,* vol. I: *Christian Self-Government* (San Francisco: The Foundation for American Christian Education, 1960), p. 266. Excerpted from Frederick D. Stone, *The Founding of Pennsylvania,* 1884, Windsor's, vol. III. Used by permission.

[5] Hawthorne, *Orations,* p. 136. "The Boston Massacre" delivered by John Hancock at Boston, March 5, 1774 after the tragic collision between British regulars and colonial dissenters occurred.

[6] Ibid., p. 22. "On the Writs of Assistance" by James Otis. Delivered before the Superior Court of Massachusetts during the term held at Boston, in February, 1761.

[7] Ibid., p. 28. "Inaugural Address" delivered by George Washington on the occasion of his first inauguration as President of the United States on April 30, 1789 in New York City.

[8] Ibid., p. 29.

[9] Ibid., pp. 32-33. "Farewell Address" delivered by George Washington on the occasion of his departure

from the second term of his presidency. Published on September 17, 1796.

[10] Ibid., p. 41.

[11] Ibid., p. 45.

[12] Rosalie June Slater in the Preface to Webster, *The American Dictionary of the English Language,* p. 12.

[13] John Wesley Hill, *Abraham Lincoln: Man of God* (New York: G.P. Putnam's Sons, 1927), p. 391.

[14] Ibid., pp. 286-287. From a discussion with Newton Bateman, Superintendent of Public Instruction for the State of Illinois concerning a ministerial vote on the issue of slavery.

[15] Jasper L. McBrien, *America First* (New York: American Book Company, 1916), pp. 195-196. From "The Duty and Value of Patriotism," a lecture delivered before the New York Commandery of the Loyal Legion, New York, April 4, 1894.

[16] Ibid., pp. 196-197.

[17] Hall, *The Christian History of the Constitution,* p. IA.

[18] Ibid., p. 183. Written by John Overton Choules in his Preface to the 1844 reprint of Neals' *History of the Puritans,* 1731.

[19] Philip Van Doren Stern, *The Life and Writings of Abraham Lincoln* (New York: The Modern Library, Random House, Inc., 1942), pp. 656-657. First inaugural Address by Abraham Lincoln, March 4, 1861.

[20] McBrien, *America First,* p. 128. Address given by Senator John W. Daniel from Virginia at the dedication of the Washington National Monument, February 21, 1885.

On the Bible

Bible, n. [Gr. *biblos*, book] The Book, by way of eminence; the sacred volume, in which are contained the revelations of God, the principles of Christian faith, and the rules of practice. It consists of two parts, called the Old and New Testaments.

The Bible should be the standard of language as well as of faith.[1]

All Scripture is inspired by God and profitable for teaching, for reproof, for correction, for training in righteousness; that the man of God may be adequate, equipped for every good work. (2 Timothy 3:16-17)

The Law of the LORD is perfect, restoring
    the soul;
The testimony of the LORD is sure, making
    wise the simple.
The precepts of the LORD are right, rejoicing the heart;
The commandment of the LORD is pure, enlightening the eyes. . . .

They are more desirable than gold, yes,
*   than much fine gold;*
Sweeter also than honey and the drippings
*   of the honeycomb.*
Moreover, by them Thy servant is warned;
In keeping them there is great reward.
(Psalm 19:7-8, 10-11)

Thy word is a lamp to my feet,
And a light to my path.
(Psalm 119:105)

The Bible—God's Holy Word. There has never been any book like it nor will there ever be. The story of its supernatural origin, compilation and preservation is enough to awe even the most severe skeptic who will objectively examine it. The New Analytical Bible, first published in 1931, sheds light on the marvel of the Bible's development:

> . . . [The] writing of the Old Testament extended through a period of 1,500 years. It represents many authors. . . . That it is very difficult to maintain unity in all of the particulars related to a great central truth, under circumstances which vary from century to century, is readily seen. . . . In the genesis and development of its Messianic idea the Bible takes us back to the beginning. . . . From the era of Abraham this central truth ran across natural lines for a period of 2,000 years. . . . The stamp of divinity rests upon it and cannot be erased by all the cavils of the skeptic. . . . To assume that such a thing has evolved as a human concept, held throughout the centuries, requires infinitely more faith than to believe in the divine authorship of the Bible. It is

either a man-made scheme or a divine plan; there is no middle ground."[2]

The light brought by the Bible has changed the course of empires. The lives of many were given defending it and protecting it for posterity. When the Bible resurfaced after being cloistered during the Dark Ages for a period of a thousand years in monasteries, the world was ripe for its life-giving precepts. Thus the great Reformation of the midmillennium sprang forth. Once the Word was in the hands of the common person, the flowering of civilization unfolded dramatically. Nothing else, save the very Word of God, could have affected the hearts of mankind in such a dynamic way so as to compel progress on every front of human experience almost simultaneously.

So deeply did the Holy Scriptures touch the soul with its wisdom and inspiration that explorers opened new worlds at its bequest; inventors developed astounding devices based upon its illumination; artists poured beauty and majesty into their works of marble and canvas as they labored by its light. Pagan Roman and barbarian governments were swept away and others were established in their places as people applied the Bible's radical view of the individual. This Christian idea of man clearly taught that the State was seen as the servant of the individual rather than the other way around. People—*all people*—were seen as uniquely created in God's image with intrinsic value (Matthew 10:29-31).

We can readily trace the history of our own republic back to 1382 when the Bible was translated into English by John Wycliffe. Once the English people had tasted of its magnificence as individuals, a steady and determined change took place in their view of themselves and the world. From the establishment of the Pilgrim congregation at Scrooby, England to the signing of the Declaration of Independence to the ratification of the United States Constitution, the imprint of the Holy Bible has been emblazoned on the founding of this nation for all to see.

The Bible is no longer considered the source of all truth and wisdom but has been relegated to the position of compendium of myths, poetry and religious narrative. How has this happened in a nation whose very soul was birthed in Holy Scripture?

With this in mind, one must ask: Where has the honor, reverence and fear of the Bible gone in our present era? How is it that we in modern America have failed to walk by its light? The guiding principles of our great land are no longer permitted to be posted on the walls of our state-sponsored schools. The Bible is no longer considered the source of all truth and wisdom by many, but has been relegated to the position of compendium of myths, poetry and religious narrative. How has this happened in a nation whose very soul was birthed in Holy Scripture?

Let us examine the words and writings of the men and women who helped establish and guide our republic by its illumination. Perhaps through their wisdom, exhortation and direction we can once again fully embrace its message and say with the psalmist: "Thy word I have treasured in my heart, that I may not sin against Thee" (Psalm 119:11).

★   ★   ★

". . . schools will prove to be great gates of hell . . ."

The Protestant Reformation of the sixteenth century was integral to the founding of our nation. In fact, it became the cornerstone of liberty around which America was built. Martin Luther elevated the Bible to the place of supreme authority in the life of the believer.

> I am much afraid that schools will prove to be great gates of hell unless they diligently labor in explaining the Holy Scriptures, engraving them in the hearts of youth. I advise no one to place his child where the Scriptures do not reign paramount. Every institution in which men are not increasingly occupied with the Word of God must become corrupt.[3]

It is tragic to see generations of American children being educated without the benefit of the Bible. No wonder our national moral compass has gone awry.

It's time to remember the value of teaching the Bible!

". . . the Bible for their own law book . . ."

John Adams, American Christian patriot and second president of the United States, recognized the value of the Bible and its power to transform lives. Adams painted a picture which reflects this hope of the founding fathers for our own nation:

> Suppose a nation in some distant region should take the Bible for their own law book, and every member should regulate his conduct by the precepts there contained! Every member would be obliged in conscience to temperance, frugality and industry; to justice, kindness and charity towards his fellow men; and to piety, love and reverence toward Almighty God.[4]

Psalm 33:12 states: "Blessed is the nation whose God is the LORD." Only by following the principles and precepts of the Bible will we enjoy the peace and brotherhood for which the world longs.

It's time to remember the effect of living by the Bible's standards!

". . . the Bible is the best book in the world . . ."

President John Adams was an avid scholar. His tenacious search for truth led him to the conclusion that the Bible was the final authority on life.

> I have examined all, as well as my narrow sphere, my straightened means, and my busy life would allow me; and the result is that the Bible is the best book in the world. It contains more of my little philosophy than all the libraries I have seen. . . .[5]

The wisdom and richness of the Bible are beyond our finite human mind and experience. In its words are revealed the very nature of God and His universe. May we embrace its teachings as we pattern our lives by its principles.

It's time to remember our final authority!

"The Bible is worth
all other books . . ."

Patrick Henry was a fiery orator and a devout Christian who took life and liberty seriously. He was elected five times as governor of Virginia, a distinctive never repeated by any other American. His view of the Bible reveals the source and depth of his convictions: "The Bible is worth all other books which have ever been printed."[6]

Patrick Henry was known for his uncompromising defense of biblical truth and morality. He stood firmly on the Bible as the source of his convictions. So let us proclaim the veracity and power of God's Word in our daily lives.

It's time to remember godly conviction!

"Those duties are to God, to your fellow-creatures, and to your self"

President John Quincy Adams had a great appreciation for the Bible. As ambassador to Russia, he wrote: "My custom is, to read four to five chapters every morning immediately after rising from my bed. It employs about an hour of my time."[7]

John Quincy Adams received his love and appreciation for God's Word from his father, John Adams. The elder Adams taught young John the importance of forming and adopting biblical principles for his own self-government and communication with others. "It is in the Bible, you must learn them, and from the Bible you must learn how to practice them. Those duties are to God, to your fellow-creatures, and to your self."[8]

At one time, the Bible provided the framework for nearly every interaction between people in our republic. Are we passing this appreciation on to our children?

It's time to remember our duties as parents!

"There never was a more sure and sublime system of morality . . ."

Perhaps of greatest controversy in the examination of the religious views of the American founders is the position of Thomas Jefferson in regard to Christianity and the Bible. Upon examination of Jefferson's life and works, one can see a definite unfolding of his views. It appears that near the end of his life he may have entertained serious questions about orthodox Christianity.

However, during the years when he was having the greatest impact on the shaping of the nation, Jefferson's ideas demonstrated a clear appreciation for the Christian Church and the Bible. Thomas Jefferson was a great friend and supporter of Bible societies and made it his business to see that God's Word was distributed widely. His appreciation for the impact of Scripture on the individual is seen in these two statements:

> I had not supposed there was a family in this State not possessing a Bible. . . . I, therefore, enclose you cheerfully, an order . . . for fifty dollars, for the pur-

poses of the [Bible] Society. . . . There never was a more pure and sublime system of morality delivered to man than is to be found in the four Evangelists. (1814, to Samuel Greenhow)[9]

The Bible is the cornerstone of liberty. A student's perusal of the sacred volume will make him a better citizen, a better father, a better husband.[10]

Jefferson's sentiments are opposed to those who today decry sound Christian standards for men, women and children. He was correct in his appraisal of the great treasure of wisdom and morality found in the Bible. Let us return God's Word to the position of central authority for all of life and learning.

It's time to remember the
"great Tutor in right living"!

". . . miseries . . . proceed from despising . . . the Bible"

Noah Webster, the remarkable "Schoolmaster of the Nation" held the Bible in highest esteem. Much of his private, public and professional writing is dedicated to the infusion of biblical principles into the life-stream of the infant nation.

> The moral principles and precepts contained in the Scriptures, ought to form the basis of all our civil constitutions and laws. . . . All the miseries and evils which men suffer from vice, crime, ambition, injustice, oppression, slavery and war, proceed from despising or neglecting the precepts contained in the Bible.[11]

The miseries and evils to which Webster referred afflict America today. He understood the connection between the well-being of a society and the degree to which that society embraces the teachings of the Bible. Do we?

It's time to remember to embrace the Bible!

"The Bible is the . . . cause of all that is good . . ."

Noah Webster saw the Bible as a practical book as well as a spiritual guide.

> The Bible is the chief and moral cause of all that is good, and the best corrector of all that is evil, in human society; the best book for regulating the temporal concerns of men, and the only book that can serve as an infallible guide for future felicity.[12]

Society, as well as the individual, can only benefit from adhering to the Bible's principles.

It's time to remember our "infallible guide"!

"So great is my veneration for the Bible . . ."

Many believe that the Bible and education don't mix—or at least that God's Word is only minimally relevant for today's learner. John Quincy Adams had a much different view. That he was a remarkable individual is without dispute. At the age of fourteen he served as ambassador to Russia, and he later became our sixth president. His words affirm the value of the Bible in education.

> So great is my veneration for the Bible that the earlier my children begin to read it the more confident will be my hope that they will prove useful citizens of their country and respectable members of society. I have for many years made it a practice to read through the Bible once every year.[13]

John Quincy Adams knew well the impact of the Bible in educating the young and preparing them for usefulness in their future stations.

It's time to remember the place of the Bible in raising children!

"It is impossible to rightly govern . . . without God and the Bible"

Historically, God's Word has been revered and frequently consulted in American public life. Many of our past presidents have taken bold stands on behalf of the importance of the Bible and its needed influence in our society. In recent history, President Ronald Reagan proclaimed 1983 as The Year of the Bible in honor of the tremendous impact and influence of this Book of books on our nation. Long ago George Washington wrote: "It is impossible to rightly govern . . . without God and the Bible."[14]

Abraham Lincoln remarked: "In regard to this Great Book, I have but to say, I believe that the Bible is the best gift God has given to man."[15]

If these great men of our past recognized the value of the Bible, how can it be that this very Book has no credibility in the classrooms of our government schools today?

It's time to remember God's gift of the Bible!

"I count that man
my worst enemy . . ."

We live at a time when the religion of humanism is prevailing on many fronts. People have become their own gods, setting their own standards upon which choices are made. There are no longer recognized absolutes of right and wrong. President James Buchanan demonstrated an obvious understanding of the human condition and our need for the truth of God's Word.

> I count that man my worst enemy who would endeavor to weaken my faith in the Bible as the very revealed Word of God, or in Jesus Christ as the atonement for sin. . . . He would take from me the only hope I have that my sinful nature may be purified, and fitted to dwell in happiness in the presence of a pure and sinless God forever.[16]

Such a view may be ridiculed by many today. That, however does not negate its truthfulness.

It's time to remember
our need for God's saving grace!

"The character of the Bible is easily established . . ."

Abraham Lincoln is one of the most honored and revered American presidents. Most children hear of his tenacious hunger for learning as a youth. Among the books that he read by candlelight in his frontier home was the Bible. Later in life, Lincoln often referred to and quoted from the Bible. There was good reason for this—he believed it.

> The character of the Bible is easily established, at least to my satisfaction. We have to believe many things which we do not comprehend. The Bible is the only history that claims to be God's Book—to comprise His laws, His history. It contains an immense amount of evidence as to its authenticity. . . . I decided a long time ago that it was less difficult to believe that the Bible was what it claimed to be than to disbelieve it.[17]

It's time to remember the character and veracity of the Bible!

"But for this book . . ."

In 1864, President Lincoln demonstrated his great love and appreciation for God's Word when acknowledging a special gift from the Committee of Colored People from Baltimore: "All the good from the Saviour of the world is communicated to us through this book. But for this book we could not know right from wrong. All those things desirable to man are contained in it."[18]

The answer to all of life's questions and the remedy for all of society's ills are still to be found within its pages!

It's time to remember the Bible is the answer!

"... I am right, ... for Christ teaches it and Christ is God"

When faced with moral dilemmas, the first place to which many of the leaders and statesmen of our nation turned was the Bible and the principles of Christianity. This is evidenced in Abraham Lincoln's assessment of the problem of slavery which was a chief political and moral question of his time.

> I know that I am right, because I know that Liberty is right, for Christ teaches it and Christ is God. I have told them that a house divided against itself cannot stand, and Christ and reason say the same, and they will find it so. ... I may not see the end, but it will come, and I shall be vindicated, and these men will find that they have not read their Bible aright.[19]

Lincoln reasoned from God's Word to the issue of slavery. The Bible has the answer for every dilemma known to man.

It's time to remember where to turn!

"The first and almost only Book deserving universal attention . . ."

In 1963, the U.S. Supreme Court banned the reading of Scripture in public school classrooms. At one time this Book was held in highest regard by nearly everyone. President John Quincy Adams stated: "The first and almost only Book deserving universal attention is the Bible."[20]
President Calvin Coolidge said:

> The foundations of our society and our government rest so much on the teaching of the Bible that it would be difficult to support them if faith in these teachings would cease to be practically universal in our country.[21]

We are a nation adrift, having lost our anchor to the Word of God. Tragically, this can be seen in the heinous acts which are commonplace today within every segment of the American population.

It's time to remember our anchor!

" . . . the Word of God has made a unique contribution in shaping the United States . . ."

A few years ago a lawsuit was brought against a public school in order to remove the Bible from its library because it was said to be obscene and might cause psychological damage. Just a mere decade before this, the United States Congress declared the praises of this Book of books in this resolution:

> WHEREAS the Bible, the Word of God, has made a unique contribution in shaping the United States as a distinctive and blessed nation of people; WHEREAS deeply held religious convictions springing from the Holy Scriptures led to the early settlement of our Nation; WHEREAS Biblical teachings inspired concepts of civil government that are contained in our Declaration of Independence and the Constitution of the United States. . . . Renewing our knowledge of, and our faith in God through the Holy Scriptures can strengthen us as a nation and a people . . . be it resolved to designate 1983 as a

national "Year of the Bible" in recognition of both the formative influence the Bible has been for our nation, and our national need to study and apply the teachings of the Holy Scriptures.[22]

It's time to remember
the biblical foundation of our nation!

For the word of God is living and active and sharper than any two-edged sword, and piercing as far as the division of soul and spirit . . . able to judge the thoughts and intentions of the heart. (Hebrews 4:12)

Notes

[1] Noah Webster, *The American Dictionary of the English Language* (1828 facsimile edition, San Francisco: The Foundation for American Christian Education, 1967; 1995). Used by permission.

[2] John A. Dickson, *The Dickson New Analytical Bible* (Iowa Falls, Iowa: World Bible Publishers, 1973), p. 1710. Used by permission.

[3] Robert Flood, *The Rebirth of America* (Philadelphia: The Arthur S. DeMoss Foundation, 1986), p. 127.

[4] Charles Francis Adams, ed., *The Works of John Adams: Second President of the United States* (Boston: Little, Brown and Company, 1856), vol. II, p. 6.

[5] Ibid., vol. X, p. 85.

[6] William Wirt, *The Life and Character of Patrick Henry* (Philadelphia: James Webster, 1818), p. 402.

[7] Verna M. Hall and Rosalie J. Slater, *The Bible and the Constitution of the United States of America* (San Francisco: Foundation for American Christian Education, 1983), p. 17. Used by permission.

[8] Ibid.

[9] Mark A. Beliles, *Thomas Jefferson's Abridgment of The Words of Jesus of Nazareth* (Charlottesville, VA: Mark A. Beliles, 1993), Introduction, p. 19. Used by permission.

[10] Ibid.

[11] Hall and Slater, *The Bible and the Constitution*, p. 28.

[12] Verna M. Hall, *The Christian History of the American Revolution: Consider and Ponder* (San Francisco: Foundation for American Christian Education, 1976), p. 21. Used by permission. Preface to The Holy Bible containing the

Old and New Testaments, in the Common Version. With Amendments of the Language, by Noah Webster, LL.D. New Haven, 1833.

[13] Verna M. Hall, *The Christian History of the Constitution of the United States of America*, vol. I: Christian Self-Government (San Francisco: The Foundation for American Christian Education, 1960), pp. 615-616.

[14] W. Herbert Burk, *Washington's Prayers* (Norristown, PA: Published for the benefit of the Washington Memorial Chapel, 1907), pp. 87-95.

[15] Paul Selby, *Lincoln's Life Stories and Speeches* (Chicago: Thompson and Thomas, 1902), p. 222.

[16] Stephen Abbot Northrop, *A Cloud of Witnesses* (Portland, OR: American Heritage Ministries, 1987), p. 57. Used by permission.

[17] Ibid., p. 286.

[18] Selby, *Lincoln's Life Stories*, p. 222.

[19] John Wesley Hill, *Abraham Lincoln: Man of God* (New York: G.P. Putnam's Sons, 1927), pp. 285-286. From a discussion with Newton Bateman, Superintendent of Public Instruction for the State of Illinois concerning a ministerial vote on the issue of slavery.

[20] Nancy Leigh DeMoss, *The Rebirth of America* (Philadelphia: Arthur S. DeMoss Foundation, 1986), p. 37.

[21] Ibid.

[22] October 4, 1982, by a Joint Resolution of the Senate and the House of Representatives in the second session of the 97th Congress. Public Law 97-280, 96 Stat. 1211.

On Character and Morality

Character, n. [L., Gr. *character*; from the verb to scrape, cut, engrave] The peculiar qualities, impressed by nature or habit on a person, which distinguish him from others; these constitute *real character*, and the qualities which he is supposed to possess constitute his *estimated character*, or reputation. Hence we say, a *character* is not formed when the person has not acquired stable and distinctive qualities.

By way of eminence, distinguished or good qualities; those which are esteemed and respected; and those which are ascribed to a person in common estimation. We inquire whether a stranger is a man of *character*.[1]

Morality, n. [Fr. *moralité*] The doctrine or system of moral duties, or the duties of men in their social character; ethics.

The practice of moral duties; virtue.

The quality of an action which renders it good; the conformity of an act to the divine law, or to the principles of rectitude. This conformity implies that the act must be performed by a free agent, and from the motive of obedience to the divine will.[2]

Blessed are the poor in spirit, for theirs is
    the kingdom of heaven.
Blessed are those who mourn, for they
    shall be comforted.
Blessed are the gentle, for they shall inherit
    the earth.
Blessed are those who hunger and thirst
    for righteousness, for they shall be
    satisfied.
Blessed are the merciful, for they shall re-
    ceive mercy.
Blessed are the pure in heart, for they shall
    see God.
Blessed are the peacemakers, for they shall
    be called sons of God.
Blessed are those who are persecuted for
    the sake of righteousness, for theirs is
    the kingdom of heaven.
(Matthew 5:3-10)

. . . applying all diligence, in your faith supply moral excellence, and in your moral excellence, knowledge; and in your knowledge, self-control, and in your self-control, perseverance, and in your perseverance, godliness; and in your godliness, brotherly kindness, and in your brotherly kindness, Christian love. For if these qualities are yours and are increasing, they render you neither useless nor unfruitful in the true knowledge of our Lord Jesus Christ. For he who lacks these qualities is blind or short-sighted, having forgotten his purification from his former sins. (2 Peter 1:5-9)

. . . but we also exult in our tribulations, knowing that tribulation brings about perseverance; and perseverance, proven character; and proven character, hope . . . (Romans 5:3-4)

God's Word clearly teaches the value of character. In Samuel's search for a new king over Israel to replace Saul, God redirected Samuel's thoughts from the typically human focus on external appearance to the more important arena of the heart. It is the internal qualities of man that will determine his outward expressions and actions. "For as he thinks within himself, so he is" (Proverbs 23:7).

As noted in Webster's definition, character is something that comes at a price. The root of this word comes from "to scrape, cut or engrave"— not exactly a pleasant prospect. There is no easy way to attain quality character. While the process is accelerated by an encounter with Jesus Christ, it is still a lifelong process. So important is character, the Bible tells us, that without growth in our character we cannot even enter the kingdom of God!

Certainly Jesus represents the greatest role model of godly character that man has ever known. In Him we see the perfect reflection of our heavenly Father. In Him we view the standard to which we should all aspire. It is through Him and by Him that we become like Him. "Therefore, if anyone is in Christ, he is a new creation; the old has gone, the new has come!" (2 Corinthians 5:17, NIV). Furthermore, one of the magnificent truths of the gospel message is that it is never too late for a fresh start. "Because of the

LORD's great love we are not consumed, for his compassions never fail" (Lamentations 3:22, NIV).

Traveling along the Chain of Christianity[3] on its westward course through history, one finds many along the way who exhibit the character of Christ. Through trials and tribulations of untold proportion, these pillars of the past stand as beacons who have let their lights "shine before men" that our Father in heaven may be glorified (see Matthew 5:16).

Jesus represents the greatest role model of godly character that man has ever known. In Him we see the perfect reflection of our heavenly Father. In Him we view the standard to which we should all aspire. It is through Him and by Him that we become like Him.

From the Pilgrims to the Presidents, the themes of virtue and morality can be readily seen in their speeches, journals and letters. Let us glean truth and hope from the wisdom of those who established the world's first Christian Constitutional Republic.

Yes, character counts! May we once again embrace the values and precepts that our forefathers held so dear. May God grant to this nation another chance to return to His standard and thus receive His blessing.

★   ★   ★

"... good laws do well, good men do better..."

Much debate has raged in recent elections over the idea of *character*. William Penn, Quaker preacher, writer and founder of the Pennsylvania colony, offered insight on this important topic over 300 years ago.

> Let men be good, and the governments cannot be bad; if it be ill they will cure it. ... Some say, let us have good laws, and no matter for the men who execute them: but let them consider, that good laws do well, good men do better. ...[4]

There is no substitute for leaders with godly character. We cannot expect a system of government to model good and noble living. We need men and women who will demonstrate the Christian principles of morality, justice, service and humility.

It's time to remember the
importance of a moral example!

". . . a virtuous education of youth . . ."

William Penn offered insight into the necessity for investing biblical values in our children:

> That, therefore, which makes a good constitution, must keep it, viz: men of wisdom and virtue, qualities, that because they descend not with worldly inheritance, must be carefully propagated by a virtuous education of youth. . . [5]

Mr. Penn understood the natural proclivity of men to do evil. In order to assure that there will be people of good character to maintain good government, we must give attention to training young people in Christian virtue.

It's time to remember to model virtue!

"... let us become a virtuous people ..."

Samuel Adams was known as the "father of the American Revolution." Mr. Adams understood the indissoluble link between the virtue of the people and the future success of our republic.

> He therefore is the truest friend to the liberty of his country who tries most to promote its virtues, and who, so far as his power and influence extend, will not suffer a man to be chosen into any office of power and trust who is not a wise and virtuous man. ... The sum of all is, if we would most truly enjoy this gift of Heaven, let us become a virtuous people. ...[6]

In a democratic republic such as America, the responsibility for the state of the nation rests largely with the voting public. We must be on guard when we listen to those who aspire to higher office. There are many who use the phrases of Christian principles and virtuous living, and yet do not act accordingly.

It's time to remember to be discerning voters!

". . . *let justice be one of its characteristics . . .*"

Character is not reserved for the individual alone. Nations too have a character which emanates from the sum total of its leaders and citizens. General George Washington understood this early in his career as he participated in the establishment of America. In 1783, in a letter to Theodorick Bland, he wrote: "We now have a National character to establish; and it is of the utmost importance to stamp favourable impressions upon it; let justice be one of its characteristics, and gratitude another."[7]

A superior example of grace and nobility of character in public service is our beloved first president. His concern for the public good is clearly demonstrated in his first inaugural address.

> To the preceding observations I have one to add. . . . It concerns myself, and will therefore be as brief as possible. When I was first honored with a call into the service of my country, then on the eve of the arduous struggle for its liberties, the light in which I contemplated my duty required that I should

renounce every pecuniary compensation. From this resolution, I have in no instance departed. And being still under the impressions which produced it, I must decline, as inapplicable to myself, any share in personal emoluments, which may be indispensably included in a permanent provision for the executive department; and must accordingly pray that the pecuniary estimates for the station in which I am placed, may, during my continuance in it, be limited to such actual expenditures as the public good may be thought to require.[8]

Washington here demonstrated the ideals of what may be considered the quintessential qualities of a public servant. He placed his own welfare *after* the public good. Using the public office as a forum for personal aggrandizement was foreign to him. Let us hold the politicians of our generation to this same standard.

It's time to remember how to be servants!

". . . we are desirous to live in amity with all mankind"

President Washington linked the character of the nation with the character of the people. In order for America to fulfill her God-given mission of lighting the way for the world, her citizens must remain true to the godly principles that made her great.

> To complete the American character, it remains for the citizens of the United States to show the world that the reproach heretofore cast on Republican governments, for their want of stability, is without foundation when that government is the deliberate choice of an enlightened people. And I am fully persuaded that every well-wisher to the happiness and prosperity of this country will evince, by his conduct, that we live under a government of laws, and that, while we preserve inviolate our national faith, we are desirous to live in amity with all mankind.[9]

It is sometimes said that people in other nations see Americans as arrogant and self-centered. Perhaps we do not adequately demonstrate Christian virtue and morality in a way that positively affects those who are observing us. Washington enjoins us to do that very thing.

> The virtue, moderation, and patriotism which marks the steps of the American people, in framing, adopting, and thus far carrying into effect our present system of government, have excited the admiration of nations. It only now remains for us to act up to those principles which should characterize a free and enlightened people, that we may gain respect abroad, and insure happiness to ourselves and our posterity.[10]

The government of the United States was unique in its founding and in the scope of its Christian message. It has been a beacon of hope for the beleaguered world. May we hold high the standard of righteousness inherent in its founding documents. May we demonstrate Christ first in all our dealings.

It's time to remember to act on principle!

". . . honesty is the best policy"

In 1796, President Washington admonished in his Farewell Address:

> Of all the dispositions and habits that lead to political prosperity, religion and morality are indispensable supports. In vain would that man claim the tribute of patriotism who should labor to subvert these great pillars of human happiness, these firmest props of the duties of men and citizens. The mere politician, equally with the pious man, ought to respect and cherish them. A volume could not trace all their connections with private and public felicity.[11]

Washington later confirms his belief that public and private morality are both necessary and required. These succinct words of wisdom would serve modern Americans and their public servants well: "I hold the maxim no less applicable to public than to private affairs, that honesty is the best policy."[12]

It's time to remember honesty!

". . . just men who will rule in the fear of God"

The citizens of a republic are accountable before God for whom they elect. Founding father Noah Webster addressed this very issue.

> . . . God commands you to choose for rulers, just men who will rule in the fear of God. The preservation of a republican government depends on the faithful charge of this duty; if the citizens neglect their duty and place unprincipled men in office, the government will soon be corrupted; . . . and the rights of the citizens will be violated. . . .
>
> If a republican government fails to secure public prosperity and happiness, it must be because the citizens neglect the divine commands, and elect bad men to make and administer the laws.[13]

Our voting decisions should be based on who aligns with the moral standards of God's Word rather than on what most benefits our wallets.

It's time to remember to choose leaders who fear God!

". . . small powers wisely and steadily directed"

Noah Webster believed that the primary method of inculcating truth and morality into youth was by way of proper education. "The Education of youth, [is] an employment of more consequence than making laws and preaching the gospel, because it lays the foundation on which both law and gospel rest for success."[14]

Mr. Webster also addressed the issue of the education of women, seeing their role as definitive in establishing the character and abilities of the rising generation. "Their own education should therefore enable them to implant in the tender mind, such sentiments of virtue, propriety and dignity, as are suited to the freedoms of governments."[15]

Noah Webster summed up the power of character in determining the success of individuals and nations: "An immense effect may be produced by small powers wisely and steadily directed."[16]

*It's time to remember
the power of a godly education!*

"Our Constitution was made only for a moral and religious people"

American presidents have a singular opportunity to speak to the moral fabric of the nation. President John Adams outlined the character necessary for the perpetuation of the republic he helped establish.

> We have no government armed with power capable of contending with human passions unbridled by morality and religion. Avarice, ambition, revenge, or gallantry, would break the strongest cords of our Constitution as a whale goes through a net. Our Constitution was made only for a moral and religious people. It is wholly inadequate to the government of any other.[17]

Surely in these perverse times we are stretching the restraining power of our Constitution to its very limits.

It's time to remember the destructive power of immorality!

> *"We have staked the whole future . . . upon the capacity of mankind for self-government . . ."*

Is the idea of character important in the grand design of American society? Do one's conduct and actions bear any consequence? James Madison, fourth president and chief architect of the U.S. Constitution, wrote:

> We have staked the whole future of American civilization, not upon the power of government, far from it. We have staked the future of all our political institutions upon the capacity of mankind for self-government; upon the capacity of each and all of us to govern ourselves, to control ourselves, to sustain ourselves according to the Ten Commandments of God.[18]

Without both the foundation and the restraint of Christian character, our American civilization will continue to unravel.

It's time to remember the Ten Commandments!

". . . lifetime goals . . ."

Benjamin Franklin is known for his popular sayings and earthy wisdom. Characterized by many as an irreverent secularist, Franklin's name is invoked as an American champion of the humanistic "Enlightenment" movement that took root in France just prior to their revolution in the late eighteenth century.

While Franklin admitted to having difficulty in accepting the divinity of Jesus Christ, he was anything but anti-Christian, as many of the French revolutionaries were. Many of his proverbs and maxims were biblical in origin if not outright paraphrases. Franklin spent a great deal of time contemplating the necessity and means for achieving a virtuous life. Here we see a list of thirteen character traits that he chose as his lifetime goals:

1. Temperance . . . drink not to elevation.
2. Silence . . . avoid trifling conversation.
3. Order: Let all your things have their places.
4. Resolution . . . perform without fail what you resolve.
5. Frugality . . . i.e., waste nothing.

6. Industry: Lose no time; be always employ'd.
7. Sincerity: Use no hurtful deceit; think innocently.
8. Justice: Wrong none by doing injuries.
9. Moderation: Avoid extremes; forbear resenting.
10. Cleanliness: Tolerate no uncleanness in body.
11. Tranquillity: Be not disturbed at trifles.
12. Chastity
13. Humility: Imitate Jesus.[19]

This list offers some of the key attributes that hallmark a civilized people. Each one has a biblical root. What a marvelous pattern for one's life.

It's time to remember to follow
a biblical framework for life!

". . . the character of a doer of good . . ."

Benjamin Franklin saw great merit in following a code of morals and treating his fellowman in a Christian manner. In a letter to the son of Puritan leader Cotton Mather, Franklin revealed his attitude about the value of character.

> I have always set a greater value on the character of a doer of good than on any other kind of reputation; and if I have been, as you seem to think, a useful citizen, the public owes the advantage of it to that book.[20]

In his autobiography, Franklin remarked frequently about the values and lessons which were instilled in him as a child. There is little that is more important than inculcating the biblical standard of morality in our children. To accomplish this, there must be adults who have embraced that very standard and live by it.

It's time to remember to uphold the Christian standard of character!

". . . practice virtue thyself, and encourage it in others"

Patrick Henry was an outspoken advocate for the true liberty that comes from knowing God and walking in His ways. He knew the importance of right character in carrying out the purposes of God in establishing this nation. In speaking of the American people, Henry exhorts:

> If they are wise, they will be great and happy. If they are of contrary character, they will be miserable. Righteousness alone can exalt them as a nation. Reader! Whoever thou art, remember this, and in thy sphere practice virtue thyself, and encourage it in others.[21]

Surely God has prospered this nation as few others. And yet we see the signs of demise and misery all around. Henry's admonishment holds the key to restoration of this great land.

It's time to remember
that righteousness exalts a nation!

"If we lose these, we are conquered indeed"

While America faces many threats to its sovereignty and security from the outside, the greatest menace comes from the deterioration of its moral fiber within. Patrick Henry recognized this peril when he wrote in 1799:

> . . . the great pillars of all government and of social life . . . [are] virtue, morality and religion. This is the armor, my friend, and this alone, that renders us invincible. These tactics we should study. If we lose these, we are conquered indeed.[22]

King David declared: "Some trust in chariots and some in horses, but we trust in the name of the LORD our God" (Psalm 20:7, NIV).

It will take more than a larger defense budget, better military preparedness and superior weapons to provide for our security.

It's time to remember the protective nature of godly character!

> "... *government without knowledge and virtue, is like a body without a soul* ..."

We do not often hear the word *virtue* used in the major debates of our day. In Noah Webster's landmark edition of his *American Dictionary of the English Language,* he listed fifteen aspects of the definition. It can be clearly seen that *virtue* is closely aligned with *wisdom.* When our founders spoke of virtue, they understood it to mean the capacity of the possessor to be wise and good in both intent and action. They referred to it often when describing the necessary constitution of the individual in the unfolding American republic.

> A republican government without knowledge and virtue, is like a body without a soul—a mass of corruption and putrefication—food for worms.
> —John Adams[23]

> I know no safe depository of the ultimate power of society, but the people themselves; and if we think them not enlightened enough to exercise their control with a wholesome discretion,

the remedy is not to take it from them, but to improve their discretion by education. With knowledge and virtue, the united efforts of ignorance and tyranny may be defied.

—Thomas Jefferson[24]

In today's world with technological advances occurring at a dizzying rate, the questions must be asked: "Do we have the *virtue* to properly use the knowledge we are gaining? Can mankind survive in a world where ethical considerations take a 'backseat' to the calculated results of scientific advancements?"

It's time to remember that knowledge requires ethics!

"... a more suitable obedience..."

On March 6, 1799, President John Adams proclaimed a *National Fast Day* in response to the inevitable corruption which characterizes the human heart:

> ... implore His pardoning mercy, through the great Mediator and Redeemer, for our past transgressions, and that through the grace of His Holy Spirit we may be disposed and enabled to yield a more suitable obedience ... that He would interpose to arrest the progress of that impiety and licentiousness in principle and practice so offensive to Himself and so ruinous to mankind; that He would make us deeply sensible that "righteousness exalteth a nation but sin is a reproach to any people."[25]

May we once again humble ourselves as a people before Almighty God and implore His forgiveness and blessings.

It's time to remember that sin offends God!

". . . no effort in favour of virtue is lost"

John Adams corresponded frequently with Thomas Jefferson on a variety of issues. In this letter, Adams makes it very clear that he believes success must be rooted in the morality of the people.

> Have you ever found in history, one single example of a Nation thoroughly corrupted that was afterwards restored to virtue? . . . And without virtue, there can be no political liberty. . . .
>
> Will you tell me how to prevent luxury from producing effeminacy, intoxication, extravagance, vice and folly? . . . I believe no effort in favour of virtue is lost.[26]

Our society has placed the attainment of wealth and comfort above the inculcation of Christian values. We can clearly see the point that Adams was making as greed, selfishness, apathy and violence increase at an alarming pace.

It's time to remember that success must be rooted in morality!

". . . *either by the Bible or by the bayonet*"

Self-government is a cornerstone of American republicanism. Speaker of the House of Representatives in the 1840s, Robert Winthrop, eloquently described this Christian concept.

> All societies of men must be governed in some way or other. The less they may have of stringent State Government, the more they must have of individual self-government. The less they rely on public law and physical force, the more they must rely on private moral restraint. Men, in a word, must necessarily be controlled either by power within them, or by a power without them; either by the Word of God, or by the strong arm of man; either by the Bible or by the bayonet.[27]

When men fail to govern themselves, the need for external control increases. The resultant loss of liberty is very difficult to regain and affects us all.

It's time to remember "private moral restraint"!

". . . people are responsible for the character of their Congress"

How important is the average citizen in the whole scope of life and liberty? President James Garfield, who served as our twentieth president for only four months before being assassinated, made this observation:

> Now more than ever before the people are responsible for the character of their Congress. If that body be ignorant, reckless, or corrupt, it is because the people tolerate ignorance, recklessness, and corruption. If it be intelligent, brave, and pure, it is because the people demand these high qualities to represent them in the national legislature . . . if the next centennial does not find us a great nation . . . it will be because those who represent the enterprise, the culture, and the morality of the nation do not aid in controlling the political forces.[28]

It's time to remember that character counts!

". . . the Ruler of the Universe will require . . . a strict account . . ."

Grover Cleveland served as both the twenty-second and twenty-fourth president of the United States. He linked the issue of citizenship with moral character.

> All must admit that the reception of the teachings of Christ results in the purest patriotism, in the most scrupulous fidelity to public trust, and in the best type of citizenship.
>
> Those who manage the affairs of government are by this means reminded that the law of God demands that they should be courageously true to the interests of the people, and that the Ruler of the Universe will require of them a strict account of their stewardship.[29]

President Cleveland recognized the influence of Christian morality on both the governor and the governed.

It's time to remember the effects of moral character on citizenship!

"They must actually do things . . ."

Sometimes men and women compromise their fundamental beliefs and values in the face of political expediency or fear of criticism. President Theodore Roosevelt offers an excellent standard for public service.

> Men who wish to work for decent politics must work practically, and yet must not swerve from their devotion to a high ideal. They must actually do things, and not merely confine themselves to criticising those who do them. . . . They must act as Americans through and through, in spirit and hope and purpose . . . while being disinterested, unselfish and generous in their dealings with others. . . .[30]

Being a leader is not about political posturing and promising. It requires true dedication to the cause of Right.

*It's time to remember to do
rather than to criticize!*

But the fruit of the Spirit is love, joy, peace, patience, kindness, goodness, faithfulness, gentleness, self-control; against such things there is no law. (Galatians 5:22-23)

Notes

[1] Noah Webster, *The American Dictionary of the English Language* (1828 facsimile edition, San Francisco: The Foundation for American Christian Education, 1967; 1995). Used by permission.

[2] Ibid.

[3] Verna M. Hall, *The Christian History of the Constitution of the United States of America:* vol. I: *Christian Self-Government* (San Francisco: The Foundation for American Christian Education, 1960), p. 6A. Used by permission. Christianity was birthed on the continent of Asia, moved westward to be developed and expanded on the continent of Europe, then westward still to its fullest expression in the civil realm on the North American continent still moving ever westward completing the great circle back to Asia. By this is all history and mankind linked together in one divine chain.

[4] Stephen McDowell, *Providential Perspective* (Charlottesville, VA: The Providence Foundation, June/July 1991, Vol. 6, No. 5), p. 5. Used by permission.

[5] Rosalie J. Slater, *Teaching and Learning America's Christian History: The Principle Approach* (San Francisco: Foundation for American Christian Education, 1965; 1993), p. 203. Used by permission. Cited from William Penn's *Frame of Government of Pennsylvania*, 1682.

[6] Hall, *The Christian History of the Constitution*, vol. I., 364B. Excerpted from W.V. Wells, *Life of Samuel Adams*, 1865.

[7] W.B. Allen, ed., *George Washington: A Collection* (Indianapolis, IN: Liberty Fund, Inc., 1988), p. 231.

[8] Julian Hawthorne, ed., *Orations of American Orators* (New York: The Colonial Press, 1900), p. 30. "Inaugural Address" delivered by George Washington on the occasion of his first inauguration as President of the United States on April 30, 1789 in New York City.

[9] Charles R. Skinner, *Manual of Patriotism* (Albany, NY: Brandow Printing Company, 1900), p. 366.

[10] Ibid.

[11] *America: Great Crises in Our History Told by Its Makers* (Chicago: Americanization Department, Veterans of Foreign Wars of the United States, 1925), pp. 223-224.

[12] Hawthorne, *Orations*, p. 44. "Farewell Address" delivered by George Washington on the occasion of his departure from the second term of his presidency. Published on September 17, 1796

[13] *History of the United States* (New Haven: Durrie & Peck, 1832), pp. 307-308.

[14] Webster, *The American Dictionary*, in the Preface: "Noah Webster: Founding Father of American Scholarship and Education," by Rosalie J. Slater, p. 12.

[15] Ibid., p. 16.

[16] Ibid., p. 11.

[17] Charles Francis Adams, ed., *The Works of John Adams: Second President of the United States* (Boston: Little, Brown, & Co., 1854), vol. IX, p. 229.

[18] Stephen K. McDowell and Mark A. Beliles, *America's Providential History* (Charlottesville, VA: Providence Press, 1988), p. 221. Used by permission.

[19] Benjamin Franklin, *The Autobiography of Benjamin Franklin* (Newton, MA: Spencer Press, 1936), pp. 104-105.

The World's Greatest Literature series.

[20] Ibid., pp. 310-311. *The World's Greatest Literature* series. A letter to Samuel Mather, May 12, 1784.

[21] In May, 1765, Patrick Henry wrote this on the back of the Stamp Act Resolves passed in the Virginia House of Burgesses. William Wirt Henry, *Patrick Henry—Life, Correspondence and Speeches* (New York: Burt Franklin, 1969), vol. I, pp. 91-93.

[22] Stephen McDowell, *Reformation Report* (Charlottesville, VA: The Providence Foundation, May 1994, vol. 6, No. 1), p. 1. Used by permission.

[23] Alexander Maitland, Esq. *The Political Instructor and Guide to Knowledge; Being a Compendium of Political Information* (Philadelphia: William Brown, 1833), Preface.

[24] Ibid.

[25] James D. Richardson, *A Compilation of the Messages and Papers of the Presidents* (New York: Bureau of National Literature, Inc., 1897), vol. I, p. 275.

[26] Adams, *The Works of John Adams,* vol. X, p. 386.

[27] McDowell, *Providential Perspective*, p. 1. Verna M. Hall, *The Christian History of the American Revolution: Consider and Ponder* (San Francisco: Foundation for American Christian Education, 1976), p. 20. Used by permission.

[28] Richardson, *A Compilation,* vol. X, p. 4596.

[29] Ibid., vol. XI, p. 5358.

[30] Skinner, *Manual of Patriotism,* p. 371.

On Christianity
and Religion

Christianity, n. [Christian, from Christ]
The religion of Christians; or the system of doctrines and precepts taught
by Christ, and recorded by the evangelists and apostles.

Whilst politicians are disputing
about monarchies, aristocracies, and re-
publics, Christianity is alike applicable,
useful and friendly to them all.[1]

Religion, n. [L. *religio*, to bind anew; *re*
and *ligo*, to bind. This word seems
originally to have signified an oath or
vow to the gods, or the obligation of
such an oath or vow, which was held
very sacred by the Romans.]

1. Religion, in its most comprehen-
sive sense, includes a belief in the being and perfections of God, in the
revelation of his will to man, in man's
obligation to obey his commands, in a
state of reward and punishment, and
in man's accountableness to God; and
also true godliness or piety of life, with

the practice of all moral duties. It therefore comprehends theology, as a system of doctrines or principles, as well as practical piety; for the practice of moral duties without a belief in a divine lawgiver, and without reference to his will or commands, is not religion.

2. Religion, as distinct from theology, is godliness or real piety in practice, consisting in the performance of all known duties to God and our fellow men, in obedience to divine command, or from love to God and his law. James 1.

3. Religion, as distinct from virtue, or morality, consists in the performance of the duties we owe directly to God, from a principle of obedience to his will. Hence we often speak of religion and virtue, as different branches of one system, or the duties of the first and second tables of the law.

Let us with caution indulge the supposition, that morality can be maintained without religion.[2]

If anyone considers himself religious and yet does not keep a tight rein on his tongue, he deceives himself and his religion is worthless. Religion that God our Father accepts as pure and faultless is this: to look after orphans and widows in their distress and to keep oneself from being polluted by the world. (James 1:26-27, NIV)

Jesus saith unto him, I am the way, the truth, and the life: no man cometh unto the Father, but by me. If ye had known me, ye should have known my Father also: and from henceforth ye know him, and have seen him. (John 14:6-7, KJV)

This is my commandment, That ye love one another, as I have loved you. Greater love hath no man than this, that a man lay down his life for his friends. (John 15:12-13, KJV)

It was the spirit of Christianity that changed the face of the ancient world. No other event has so impacted the human race as did the coming to earth of Jesus, the Christ. So dramatic was the collision of His message with the pagan worldview of that day that it turned the world upside down within a few hundred years. By becoming a man, Christ affirmed the dignity of the individual made in God's image.

It was the kindly influence of Christianity that civilized the world. The idea that government and the State were made for the individual, not the individual for the State, threatened the very core of the established power systems of the day. Through Jesus, God's law was written on the heart of the individual, the capacity for self-government under God was restored and true liberty was experienced—first internally in the heart, then externally in the civil realm.

So substantial was the influence of the Christian religion on the establishment of America that one must conclude that without Christianity there would be no America as we know it today.[3] Although a few of the American founders did not embrace every tenet of evangelical Christianity, they had such a great appreciation of the merits and effects of Christianity that they still wrote often concerning it. In fact, far into our history as a nation, American leaders affirmed our dependence upon the biblical principles of Christianity and acknowledged their role in shaping us. No one can erase or diminish the imprint of Christianity on America without rewriting our history. Its mark is indelible, for it is the very lifeblood of our republic.

No other event has so impacted the human race as did the coming to earth of Jesus, the Christ. So dramatic was the collision of His message with the pagan worldview of that day that it turned the world upside down within a few hundred years. Jesus affirmed the dignity of the individual made in God's image.

From its earliest roots America was seen as a great tool in the hand of God for the purpose of shining and spreading the light of Christianity to the world. That America has this "gospel purpose" would be ridiculed in many segments of today's society. This idea is unmistakably clear, however, as we read the charters, founding documents and journals of the men and women who God used to plant the seeds of our great nation. From Christopher Columbus to the Virginia Charter to the Mayflower Compact, this missionary emphasis is boldly proclaimed.

> Lastly, (and which was not the least,) a great hope & inward zeall they had of laying some good foundation, or at

least to make some way thereunto, for
ye propagating & advancing ye gospell
of ye kingdom of Christ in those re-
mote parts of ye world: yea, though
they should be but even as stepping-
stones unto others for ye performing of
so great a work.[4]

The opening lines of the Mayflower Compact
leave little doubt as to the religious purpose of
the Pilgrims' voyage to the New World.

In ye name of God, Amen. We whose
names are underwritten, the loyall subjects of our dread soveraigne Lord,
King James . . . having undertaken, for
ye glory of God, and advancemente of
ye Christian faith, and honour of our
king & countrie, a voyage to plant ye
first colonie in ye Northerne parts of
Virginia, doe by these presents sol-
emnly & mutualy in ye presence of
God, and one of another, covenant &
combine ourselves together in a civill
body politick. . . ."[5]

We must regain this understanding of the
spiritual calling of America if we are to see her
continue to prosper internally and affect the
world with a Christian witness.

★   ★   ★

"... inculcating in the minds of youth the fear and love of the deity ..."

Samuel Adams, Father of the American Revolution, beautifully summarized the full scope and significance of Christianity in both the establishment of this nation and in the education of its children. In fact, Adams saw Christian education as the key to sustaining the new, *biblical* world order that was being established by God.

> Let divines and philosophers, statesmen and patriots, unite their endeavors to renovate the age, by impressing the minds of men with the importance of educating their little boys and girls, of inculcating in the minds of youth the fear and love of the deity and universal philanthropy, and, in subordination to these great principles, the love of their country; of instructing them in the art of self-government, without which they never can act a wise part in the government of societies, great or small; in short, of leading them in the study and practice of the exalted virtues of the Christian system.[6]

We cannot remove Christ and the Bible from education and expect our civilization to prosper.

It's time to remember to raise our children in a wholly Christian manner!

". . . its brightest ornament and its best security"

Movies and television have done much to malign the position of religion in our society. Samuel Adams believed that virtue and morality emanated from piety—the living expression of religion.

> I could say a thousand things to you, if I had leisure. I could dwell on the importance of piety and religion, of industry and frugality, of prudence, economy, regularity and even Government, all of which are essential to the well being of a family. But I have not time. I cannot however help repeating piety, because I think it is indispensable. Religion in a family is at once its brightest ornament and its best security.[7]

We must once again elevate the role of religion in our families and institutions. It is from its seeds that the good and noble fruit of godly character will grow in our nation.

It's time to remember to raise Christian families!

". . . an engine of policy . . ."

That great atrocities have been perpetrated in the name of religion cannot be denied. Samuel Adams expounded on this issue:

> And if we now cast our eyes over the nations of the earth we shall find, that instead of possessing the pure religion of the gospel, they may be divided either into infidels who deny the truth, or politicians who make religion a stalking horse for their ambition, or professors, who walk in the trammels of orthodoxy, and are more attentive to the traditions and ordinances of men than to the oracles of truth.
>
> The civil magistrate has everywhere contaminated religion by making it an engine of policy. . . . [8]

Let us beware of those who would contaminate the message of the true gospel and use it to manipulate or serve personal ambitions.

*It's time to remember to use
the gospel for God's purposes!*

"Atheism is unknown there . . ."

Benjamin Franklin wrote many pamphlets and articles describing what life was like in the new nation. His appreciation for the influence of Christianity on American society is noteworthy.

> . . . serious religion, under its various denominations, is not only tolerated, but respected and practised. Atheism is unknown there; infidelity rare and secret. . . . And the divine Being seems to have manifested His approbation of the mutual forbearance and kindness with which the different sects treat each other, by the remarkable prosperity with which He has been pleased to favor the whole country.[9]

What a fascinating description of a nation founded upon Christian principles. Sadly, inroads made by athiests into our public institutions have been catastrophic, while Christians have been fractionalized and are busy devouring one another (Galatians 5:15).

It's time to remember that we are one!

". . . these firmest props of the destinies of men . . ."

George Washington believed strongly that religion must be foundational in the successful planting and growth of our nation.

> Of all the dispositions and habits, which lead to political prosperity, religion and morality are indispensable supports. In vain would that man claim the tribute of patriotism, who should labor to subvert these great pillars of human happiness, these firmest props of the destinies of men and citizens. The mere politician, equally with the pious man, ought to respect and to cherish them. . . . Reason and experience both forbid us to expect, that national morality can prevail in the exclusion of religious principles.[10]

A great lesson for today. Without the influence of Christianity, we will fail in every attempt to truly reform society.

It's time to remember our Christian foundation!

*". . . God . . . graciously
held him in his hand . . ."*

This account of George Washington's obvious commitment to Christ sets him as a role model of highest standing for us to emulate.

> . . . His Excellency General Washington rode around among his army yesterday and admonished each and every one to fear God, to put away the wickedness that has set in and become so general, and to practice the Christian virtues. . . . This gentleman . . . respects God's Word, believes in the atonement through Christ, and bears himself in humility and gentleness. Therefore the Lord God has also . . . marvelously . . . preserved him from harm in the midst of countless perils, ambuscades, fatigues, etc. and has hitherto graciously held him in his hand as a chosen vessel.[11]

May we walk with the same Christian character demonstrated by Washington.

It's time to remember to imitate Christ!

"This is genuine Christianity . . ."

American educator and historian Noah Webster taught about the influence of Christianity on the world and government in his *Advice to the Young.*

> Almost all civil liberty now enjoyed in the world owes its origin to the principles of the Christian religion. . . . By the principles of the Christian religion we are not to understand the decisions of ecclesiastical councils, for they are the opinions of mere men. . . . No, the religion which has introduced civil liberty, is the religion of Christ and his apostles, which enjoins humility, piety, and benevolence; which acknowledges in every person a brother, or a sister, and a citizen with equal rights. This is genuine Christianity, and to this we owe our free constitutions of government.[12]

Webster goes on to expound the virtues of Christianity and its power to transform the world.

If men would universally cultivate these religious affections and virtuous dispositions, with as much diligence as they cultivate human science and re-finement of manners, the world would soon be a terrestrial paradise.[13]

For all the many marvelous discoveries and accomplishments of modern science, the world continues to slide into dark despair. Noah Webster was correct in his assessment. Only Christ can provide the truly abundant life.

*It's time to remember Who
has transforming power!*

"... *this sagacious injunction* ..."

In his inaugural address, second president John Adams laid out a long list of matters which he felt were the essentials of the government of the American republic. Among those cited was the role of religion, in particular, of Christianity.

> ... and with humble reverence, I feel it my duty to add, if a veneration for the religion of a people, who profess and call themselves Christians, and a fixed resolution to consider a decent respect for Christianity among the best recommendations for public service, can enable me, in any degree, to comply with your wishes, it shall be my strenuous endeavor that this sagacious injunction of the two Houses shall not be without effect.[14]

Those who are Christians need offer no apologies if they serve in public office. In fact, it is a most desirable state of affairs.

It's time to remember the role of religion!

". . . *indiscriminate contempt of all religion whatever . . .*"

President John Quincy Adams clearly established the fact that it is the presence of religion that brings happiness and fulfillment, not its absence.

> Happy, thrice happy the people of America! whose gentleness of manners and habits of virtue are still sufficient to reconcile the enjoyment of their natural rights, with peace and tranquillity of their country; whose principles of religious liberty did not result from an indiscriminate contempt of all religion whatever.... [15]

There are some today who would expunge religion altogether from public life. They lobby more for freedom *from* religion rather than *for* religious freedom. Let us beware of such subversion and embrace Mr. Adams' wise sentiments.

It's time to remember the danger of neglecting religion!

". . . I then and there consecrated myself to Christ"

Abraham Lincoln came to realize that Christianity was not just a philosophical position or a code of ethics. He encountered the supernatural renovation inherent in a personal relationship with Jesus Christ.

> When I left Springfield I asked the people to pray for me; I was not a Christian; when I buried my son, the severest trial of my life, I was not a Christian; when I went to Gettysburg and saw the graves of thousands of our soldiers, I then and there consecrated myself to Christ.[16]

Gettysburg was a watershed for Lincoln. Faced with the vestiges of the tremendous suffering and conflagration of the human struggle, Lincoln's response was to totally commit himself to the God he knew held the key to all men's destinies.

It's time to remember Who holds the keys to our lives!

". . . he had lost confidence in everything but God . . ."

The view that Lincoln was a religious skeptic and infidel was widely circulated by a few of his contemporaries who survived him, the chief being his former law partner, William Herndon. The response to these allegations was strong, swift and decisive by those who had intimate knowledge of him. One such reply was made by the Rev. Dr. Gurley, Lincoln's Washington pastor and friend.

> I do not believe a word of it. It would not have been true of him while he was here, for I have had frequent and intimate conversations with him on the subject of the Bible and of the Christian religion, when he could have had no motive to deceive me, and I consider him sound, not only in the truths of the Christian religion, but on all the fundamental doctrines and teachings; and more than that, in the later days of his chastened and weary life, after the death of his son Willie and his visit to the battlefield of Gettysburg, he said, with tears in his eyes, that he had lost

confidence in everything but God, and
that he now believed his heart was
changed and that he loved the Saviour.[17]

After speaking at length with an acquain-
tance connected with the Christian Commission concerning what constitutes a true
religious experience, President Lincoln replied,

. . . I think I can safely say that I know
of that change of which you speak; and
I will further add, that it has been my
intention for some time, at a suitable
opportunity, to make a public religious
profession.[18]

In today's secular and irreligious society,
some have tried to discount the beliefs and values held by our founding fathers and other
great American heroes. The evidence, however,
speaks volumes to the contrary.

It's time to remember the faith of our fathers!

"Knowledge is power, but it may be power for evil . . ."

Christian pastors played a tremendous and invaluable role in the founding of America and in educating its people on the biblical principles of civil liberty and government. Sermons were often themed to relate to events that were occurring in the life of the nation. One such occasion was the 100th anniversary of the Declaration of Independence. The Reverend Samuel A. Foljambe spoke eloquently about the role of Christianity on our founding in his sermon "The Hand of God in the Founding of America," reprinted in Verna Hall's *The Christian History of the American Revolution*.

> Intelligence, however, is not alone indispensable. Knowledge is power, but it may be power for evil as much as for good; it has no moral quality itself. The greatest danger of the Republic is its educated, experienced, cultivated, corrupt demagogues. Intelligence without religion is a dangerous pilot for the ship of state. Eliminate that element; take religious thought, sentiment, and aspiration from the atmosphere of our

education, and men will soon become animalized and this government will soon sink into the green pool of its own corruption. It was an instinct of self-preservation that incorporated in the Bill of Rights that "religion, morality, and knowledge are necessary to good government."[19]

On every hand we see evidence of the truth of Foljambe's observations. Scandals and corruption at the highest level of government, an educational system that is impotent to inculcate truth and inspiration into our children, and a nation divided along racial and economic lines all attest to America's need to return to its foundation of religion and biblical morality.

It's time to remember that knowledge apart from Christ can be dangerous!

". . . the common fatherhood of God and the universal brotherhood of man"

The principles of liberty which so characterize America are Christian through and through. The Old World could not rise above the fetters of a pagan philosophy that placed man beneath the sovereignty of the State and at odds with his fellows. Christ changed all that when He came with His doctrine of the value of the individual created in the image of God. The Archbishop of Saint Paul, John Ireland, lectured on this important theme in 1894:

> Slowly, amid sufferings and revolutions, humanity had been reaching out toward a reign of the rights of man. Ante-Christian paganism had utterly denied such rights. It allowed nothing to man as man; he was what wealth, place, or power made him. Even the wise Aristotle taught that some men were intended by nature to be slaves and chattels. The sweet religion of Christ proclaimed aloud the doctrine of the common fatherhood of God and the universal brotherhood of man.[20]

The archbishop continued to expound on the influence of Christianity on the world.

> Eighteen hundred years, however, went by, and the civilized world had not yet put its civil and political institutions in accord with its spiritual faith. The Christian Church was all this time leavening human society and patiently awaiting the promised fermentation. This came at last, and it came in America.[21]

There are those today who see no connection between the liberties we enjoy in America and the blessings of Christianity. It took nearly two millennia for mankind to reap the harvest of the Christian seeds sown in the first century. Let us beware that we do not, in a few generations, undo all that has been gained and paid for with so dear a price. Christianity is the greatest friend to the future felicity of our nation.

> *It's time to remember the blessings*
> *Christianity brought to our country!*

> "... the glory of America
> is that she is a great
> spiritual conception ... "

President Woodrow Wilson realized that America's greatness was not based upon its external wealth and power, but upon a deeper underlying principle.

> I would not feel any exhilaration in belonging to America if I did not feel that she was something more than a rich and powerful nation. I should not feel proud to be in some respects and for a little while her spokesman if I did not believe that there was something else than physical force behind her. I believe that the glory of America is that she is a great spiritual conception and that in the spirit of her institutions dwells not only her distinction but her power. The one thing that the world cannot permanently resist is the moral force of great and triumphant convictions.[22]

Where are our convictions today? Have we lost sight of that which is noble and right and good? Have Americans turned from their reliance on the moral principles of truth as espoused by biblical Christianity? Are we relying on our own strength, intelligence and prosperity? If, as President Wilson believed, it was our spiritual convictions that made America great, then we dare not abandon the old path. We must return to our Christian roots. There is too much at stake to do anything else.

It's time to remember
what made America great!

For no man can lay a foundation other than the one which is laid, which is Jesus Christ. (1 Corinthians 3:11)

Notes

1 Noah Webster, *The American Dictionary of the English Language* (1828 facsimile edition, San Francisco: The Foundation for American Christian Education, 1967; 1995). Used by permission.

2 Ibid.

3 Rosalie J. Slater and Verna M. Hall, *Rudiments of America's Christian History and Government: Student Handbook* (San Francisco: Foundation for American Christian Education, 1968; 2nd ed., 1994), p. 1. Used by permission.

4 Verna M. Hall, *The Christian History of the Constitution of the United States of America,* vol. I: *Christian Self-Government* (San Francisco: The Foundation for American Christian Education, 1960), p. 193. Used by permission.

5 Ibid., p. 204.

6 Ibid., p. xiv. Samuel Adams made this speech in Boston on October 4, 1790.

7 Verna M. Hall, *The Christian History of the American Revolution: Consider and Ponder* (San Francisco: Foundation for American Christian Education, 1976), p. 82. Used by permission. From *The Writings of Samuel Adams,* edited by Henry Cushing, vol. 4, New York, 1908.

8 Julian Hawthorne, ed., *Orations of American Orators* (New York: The Colonial Press, 1900), pp. 14-15. "American Independence" by Samuel Adams, delivered at the State House, Philadelphia, August 1, 1776.

9 Benjamin Franklin, "American Characteristics," *America* (Chicago: Veterans of Foreign Wars of the United States, 1925), vol. IV, p. 76.

10 Hawthorne, *Orations,* p. 40. "Farewell Address" de-

livered by George Washington on the occasion of his departure from the second term of his presidency. Published on September 17, 1796.

[11] Hall, *The Christian History of the American Revolution,* p. 68. From *The Journals of Henry Melchior Muhlenberg,* vol. III. Translated by Theodore G. Tappert and John W. Doberstein.

[12] Ibid., p. 255. From *History of the United States* by Noah Webster, New Haven, 1833.

[13] Ibid., p. 256.

[14] Hawthorne, *Orations,* p. 54. "Inaugural Address" delivered by John Adams before both houses of Congress.

[15] Hall, *The Christian History of the American Revolution,* p. 612. From *The Writings of John Quincy Adams,* edited by Worthington Chauncey Ford, 1913, p. 98.

[16] John Wesley Hill, *Abraham Lincoln: Man of God* (New York: G.P. Putnam's Sons, 1927), p. 276.

[17] Ibid., pp. 293-295.

[18] Paul Selby, *Lincoln's Life Stories and Speeches* (Chicago: Thompson and Thomas, 1902), pp. 222-223.

[19] Hall, *The Christian History of the American Revolution,* p. 53.

[20] Jasper L. McBrien, *America First* (New York: American Book Company, 1916), p. 199. From "The Duty and Value of Patriotism," a lecture delivered by John Ireland, Archbishop of Saint Paul, Minnesota, before the New York Commandery of the Loyal Legion, New York, April 4, 1894.

[21] Ibid.

[22] McBrien, *America First,* p. 82. From an address delivered by President Woodrow Wilson at the celebration of the twenty-fifth anniversary of the Daughters of the American Revolution, October 11, 1915.

On God and Providence

God, n. The Supreme Being; Jehovah; the eternal and infinite spirit, the creator, and the sovereign of the universe.

God is a spirit; and they that worship him, must worship him in spirit and in truth. John 4.[1]

Pro' vidence, n. [L. *providentia*] In theology, the care and superintendence which God exercises over his creatures. He that acknowledges a creation and denies a providence, involves himself in a palpable contradiction; for the same power which caused a thing to exist is necessary to continue its existence. Some persons admit a general providence, but deny a particular providence, not considering that a general providence consists of particulars. A belief in divine providence, is a source of great consolation to good men. By divine providence is often understood God himself.[2]

Nature, n. [L. from *nature,* born, produced]

1. In a general sense, whatever is made or produced; a word that comprehends all the works of God; the universe. Of a phoenix we say, there is no such thing in nature.

And look through *nature* up to *nature's* God. —Pope

2. By a metonymy of the effect for the cause, nature is used for the agent, creator, author, producer of things, or for the powers that produce them. By the expression, trees and fossils are produced by nature, we mean, they are formed or produced by certain inherent powers in matter, or we mean that they are produced by God, the Creator, the Author of whatever is made or produced. The opinion that things are produced by inherent powers of matter, independent of a supreme intelligent author, is atheism. But generally men mean by nature, thus used, the Author of created things, or the operation of his power.[3]

"Can I not, O house of Israel, deal with you as this potter does?" declares the LORD. "Behold, like the clay in the potter's hand, so are you in My hand, O house of Israel. At one moment I might speak concerning a nation or concerning a kingdom to uproot, to pull down, or to destroy it, if that nation against which I have spoken turns from its evil, I will relent concerning the calamity I planned to bring on it." (Jeremiah 18:6-8)

Are not two sparrows sold for a cent? And yet not one of them will fall to the ground apart from your Father. But the very hairs of your head are all numbered. Therefore do not fear; you are of more value than many sparrows. (Matthew 10:29-31)

From the founding of our nation, a majority of the American people have expressed belief in a Supreme Being. Most acknowledge this Being as the God of the Bible. Few would dispute that He was involved in the creation of the earth and all its inhabitants—despite the harangue proclaimed in the name of evolution, that illegitimate offspring of science.

Beyond this, Americans have been particularly sensitive to the still, small voice of the Heavenly Father as He beckons each individual to experience His hand in the civil realm. The founding fathers and other statesmen-leaders throughout our history have clung tenaciously to the view that God is quite active in the affairs of mankind. The humanistic philosophy of the Enlightenment was diametrically opposed to the biblical worldview that so greatly influenced the founding of the American republic.

There have been those who have tried to insinuate that major inroads were made by Deism and Universalism into the nation's religious and philosophical underpinnings at the expense of orthodox Christianity. The facts from the founding period, however, do not support such a conclusion. While some of the founders were by no means evangelical Christians as we define them today, they nonetheless had a keen appreciation for the sovereignty of God and His numerous interventions into the affairs of men. One of the most favored and prevalent names used for the deity at that time illustrates this clearly: "Providence." That America was established and protected by direct intervention of Almighty God was attested to frequently by even the most secular spokesmen.

It was this doctrine of divine providence—understanding of the nature of God and His intimate association with His creation—that brought great hope and comfort to all who accepted its truth. In the 1960s there was a popular expression, "God is dead." As we look back on that turbulent time, we see prayer and Bible reading stamped out of our public schools. We see the sexual revolution. We see respect for authority undermined and trampled upon. Can we honestly say that we are better off today than we were prior to that rebellion? Is America a nobler, freer, fairer land in which to live? Certainly, the answer is a resounding "no!"

The challenge today is to restore the memory of God's hand in our history. As young and old alike see the fear and reverence our forefathers

To know God is to know that He has a plan for the universe and for each individual. Both are governed by His laws and principles. In order to scale the heights of human potential, we must first come to terms with the living God.

had for their God, they will once again see that He is not merely the proverbial watchmaker who has wound up the universe and is passively, uncaringly allowing it to wind down. To know God is to know that He has a plan for the universe and for each individual. Both are governed by His laws and principles. In order to scale the heights of human potential, we must first come to terms with the living God. Let this begin today!

The men and women who God ordained to establish this nation understood the right relationship of man to God and to His authority. Samuel Adams, noted statesman of the Revolution, professed his grasp of this shortly after our independence was declared.

> We have this day restored the Sovereign, to whom alone men ought to be obedient. He reigns in Heaven, and with a propitious eye beholds his subjects assuming that freedom of thought, and dignity of self-direction which He bestowed on them. From the rising to the setting sun, may His kingdom come.[4]

Liberty and self-determination are gifts of God. He desires all to walk in their light. He has provided the way; now it is for to us to walk in it.

★   ★   ★

" . . . *to thy name be the praise*"

Samuel Adams fully realized the marvelous hand of intervention on behalf of the fledgling nation. His thanks and praise belong to God, and to God alone.

> And, brethren and fellow-countrymen, if it was ever granted to mortals to trace the designs of Providence, and interpret its manifestations in favor of their cause, we may, with humility of soul, cry out, Not unto us, not unto us, but to thy name be the praise. The confusion of the devices among our enemies, and the rage of the elements against them, have done almost as much towards our success as either our councils or our arms.[5]

It was not the military prowess of the colonists, not the superior minds of the leaders and not even chance that brought the miraculous conclusion of the American War for Independence. It was their Almighty God.

It's time to remember to Whom
we owe our nation!

". . . my fervent supplications to that Almighty Being . . ."

President George Washington exemplified the prevailing sentiments of the founders toward God. They believed that He was concerned not only about the physical world in which they lived, but with the character of people. Only when their hearts are right with God will people be truly fulfilled and happy.

> . . . it would be particularly improper to omit in this first official act, my fervent supplications to that Almighty Being who rules over the universe—who presides in the councils of nations—and whose providential aids can supply every human defect, that his benediction may consecrate to the liberties and happiness of the people of the United States. . . .[6]

External civil liberty begins with internal spiritual liberty. It is the truth of the cross of Christ that will set people free.

It's time to remember the Founder of all liberty!

"... he has been pleased to favor the American people ..."

George Washington cared deeply for his country. In fact, he poured out his very life on its behalf. As he was ready to leave public service, he traced out his hopes, admonishments and advice in his Farewell Address. This statement represented his acknowledgment of the sovereign power and influence of the Almighty in both the establishment and the future success of America.

> Having thus imparted to you my sentiments, as they have been awakened by the occasion which brings us together, I shall take my present leave; but not without resorting once more to the benign Parent of the human race, in humble supplication, that since he has been pleased to favor the American people, with opportunities for deliberating in perfect tranquillity, and dispositions for deciding with unparalleled unanimity on a form of government, for the security of their union, and the advancement of their happiness; so his divine blessing may be equally con-

spicuous in the enlarged views, the temperate consultations, and the wise measures on which the success of this government must depend.[7]

President Washington had no trouble recognizing and proclaiming the true way to national security. It is the blessing of God and the prayers of countless patriots who have gone before us that preserve our present liberties.

> *It's time to remember from*
> *Whom our blessings flow!*

". . . may the Being who is supreme . . ."

John Adams echoed the view held by many of the founders as he named several defining attributes of God in his inaugural address.

> And may the Being who is supreme over all, the patron of order, the fountain of justice, and the protector, in all ages of the world, of virtuous liberty, continue his blessing upon this nation and its government, and give it all possible success and duration, consistent with the ends of his providence.[8]

There was no hint of humanistic aggrandizement in President Adams' assessment of wherein the future success of America lay. Let us agree with his humble prayer of supplication on behalf of our nation.

It's time to remember to pray for our nation!

"... *he ought to be worshiped* ..."

Ben Franklin, renowned for his wit and wisdom, had a profound respect for the tenets of biblical Christianity. Of note is his knowledge of the nature and character of God. While we may never know his final decision concerning Jesus Christ in this life, we can still merit from his providential view:

> That there is one God, who made all things.
> That he governs the world by his providence.
> That he ought to be worshiped by adoration, prayer, and thanksgiving.
> But that the most acceptable service to God is doing good to man.
> That the soul is immortal.
> And that God will certainly reward virtue and punish vice, either here or hereafter.[9]

In his autobiography, Benjamin Franklin exposed his deepest thoughts and aspirations. No small part of his story was associated with his concern for the things of God.

And conceiving God to be the fountain of wisdom, I thought it right and necessary to solicit his assistance for obtaining it; to this end I formed the following little prayer, which was fixed to my tables of examination for daily use:

"O powerful Goodness! bountiful Father! merciful Guide! increase in me that wisdom which discovers my truest interest. Strengthen my resolution to perform what that wisdom dictates. Accept my kind offices to Thy other children as the only return in my power for Thy continual favors to me."[10]

In this heartfelt prayer we see the dual nature of our relationship with God as taught by Moses and Jesus. Our first allegiance is vertical—to God; our second is horizontal—to our fellow beings. This biblical concept of duality in relationship was incorporated governmentally into our federal republic by the founders.

It's time to remember
to love God and our neighbors!

*". . . let us humbly commit our
righteous cause to the great
Lord of the universe . . ."*

Most know the name of John Hancock as
the oversized, boldly scripted, first signature on the American Declaration of Independence. Few know of the character and influence of this potent patriot. Hancock held the common view of the times—that it is God who rules in the affairs of men.

> I have the most animating confidence that the present noble struggle for liberty will terminate gloriously for America. And let us play the man for our God, and for the cities of our God; while we are using the means in our power, let us humbly commit our righteous cause to the great Lord of the universe, who loveth righteousness and hateth iniquity. And having secured the approbation of our hearts, by a faithful and unwearied discharge of our duty to our country, let us joyfully leave our concerns in the hands of Him who raiseth up and pulleth down the empires and kingdoms of the world as

he pleases; and with cheerful submission to his sovereign will, devoutly say, "Although the fig-tree shall not blossom, neither shall fruit be on the vines; the labor of the olive shall fail, and the field shall yield no meat; the flock shall be cut off from the fold, and there shall be no herd in the stalls; yet we will rejoice in the Lord, we will joy in the God of our salvation."[11]

John Hancock had his priorities straight. What a noble character for our children to emulate.

It's time to remember that God controls our future!

". . . morality and piety without which social happiness cannot exist . . ."

President John Adams recognized that the success of America depended upon the continued favor of God.

> . . . the safety and prosperity of nations ultimately and essentially depend upon the protection and the blessing of Almighty God, and the national acknowledgment of this truth is not only an indispensable duty which we owe to Him, but a duty whose natural influence is favorable to the promotion of that morality and piety without which social happiness cannot exist nor the blessings of free government be enjoyed. . . .[12]

". . . Where the spirit of the Lord is, there is liberty" (2 Corinthians 3:17).

It's time to remember that we depend on the favor of God!

". . . imploring mercy . . . on our
country demands at this time
a special attention . . ."

President Adams identified the precarious predicament in which the nation was caught regarding the continuing struggles with Great Britain. He also offered a solution.

> . . . the just judgments of God against prevalent iniquity, are a loud call to repentance and reformation; and the United States of America are in a hazardous and afflictive situation. . . . It has appeared to me that the duty of imploring mercy and benediction of Heaven on our country demands at this time a special attention from its inhabitants.[13]

Mr. Adams then called for a day of humiliation, fasting and prayer—a timely remedy for our present troubles.

It's time to remember to humble
ourselves in prayer!

*". . . humiliation and prayer
be accompanied by
fervent thanksgiving . . ."*

President John Adams charged the American people to give thanks to the Lord for what He has wrought.

> . . . I recommend that . . . the duties of humiliation and prayer be accompanied by fervent thanksgiving to the Bestower of Every Good Gift, not only for His having hitherto protected and preserved the people of these United States in the independent enjoyment of their religious and civil freedom, but also for having prospered them in a wonderful progress of population, for conferring on them many great favors conducive to the happiness and prosperity of a nation.[14]

Recognizing God's hand in our lives and thanking Him is an important step for spiritual restoration.

It's time to remember to give thanks!

". . . that Being in whose hands we are . . ."

In his second inaugural address, Thomas Jefferson concluded with an appeal to God for help. Whether Jefferson ever accepted Christ as Savior, we will probably never know in this life. However, it is quite obvious that in many areas he demonstrated a biblical worldview.

> I shall need, too, the favor of that Being in whose hands we are, who . . . has covered our infancy with His providence and our riper years with His wisdom and power, and to whose goodness I ask you to join in supplications with me that He will so enlighten the minds of your servants, guide their councils, and prosper their measures that whatsoever they do shall result in your good, and shall secure you to the peace, friendship, and approbation of all nations.[15]

Let us pray for our leaders. May they recognize the God of our history and call out to Him for strength and wisdom in our present troubles.

It's time to remember to pray for our leaders!

"May we ever be under the divine guidance . . ."

Just prior to the start of the American Civil War, President James Buchanan, in his Third Annual Message, remembers the providence of God in the first 200 years of our past. He had great hope that the Lord would spare this nation once again.

> Our deep and heartfelt gratitude is due to that Almighty Power which has bestowed upon us such varied and numerous blessings throughout the past year. . . . Indeed, notwithstanding our demerits, we have much reason to believe from past events in our history that we have enjoyed the special protection of Divine Providence ever since our origin as a nation. We have been exposed to many threatening and alarming difficulties in our progress, but on each successive occasion the impending cloud has been dissipated at the moment it appeared ready to burst upon our head, and the danger to our institutions has passed away. May we ever be under the divine guidance and protection.[16]

Many people of that time were caught up in the heated debates which consumed the nation. Their concern was for their rights and their prosperity. They assumed that God would continue to bless them and avert a disaster. There comes a time, however, when God must discipline those He loves and pour out His judgment on sin. We cannot live on yesterday's visitation. Now is the time for America to humble herself before God.

It's time to remember that God punishes sin!

". . . no pen can describe the wonderful variety . . ."

Do we appreciate the abundance and blessings of our country? The glories of America can be ascribed to none other than God Himself. John Sherman spoke this truth eloquently: "No words can depict, no pen can describe, the wonderful variety, richness, grandeur and beauty which the Almighty has stamped upon this, our favored land."[17]

It is the providence of God that is the source of the geography and natural resources of this continent. The earth is a gift from God over which man has been made chief steward. It is not to be worshiped, nor is it to be abused. Let us keep a biblical perspective on our relationship to our environment. It is the home God has provided for us; the stage upon which His story for humanity is being performed.

It's time to remember our stewardship of the earth!

". . . no people . . . can prosper without His favour . . ."

In today's climate of toleration of nearly everything except Christianity, most public officials and politicians will not even mention the name of Jesus Christ. The fear of offense has caused many to forgo their most sacred property: their conscience. It was not always so in America. This Senate resolution openly acknowledged the lordship of Jesus Christ and appealed to Americans to seek God's favor in response to the dire situation in which they found themselves.

> Resolved, That, devoutly recognizing the supreme authority and just government of Almighty God in the affairs of men and of Nations, and sincerely believing that no people, however great, in numbers and resources, or however strong in the justice of their cause, can prosper without His favour, and at the same time deploring the National offenses which provoked His righteous judgment yet encouraged, in this day of trouble, by the assurance of His Word, to seek Him for succour accord-

ing to His appointed way, through Jesus Christ, the Senate do hereby request the President of the United States by his proclamation to designate and set apart a day for National prayer and humiliation, requesting all the people of the land to suspend their secular pursuits and unite in keeping the day in solemn communion with the Lord of Hosts. . . . (U.S. Senate, 1863, via Senator Harlan of Iowa—with no dissenting votes!)[18]

Jesus Christ is the way, the truth and the life. There is no other way to God. There is no other way to lasting peace. Jesus said that if we deny Him before man, He will deny us before the Heavenly Father. May we never apologize for our faith in Jesus Christ.

*It's time to remember to seek
the Prince of Peace!*

"... those Nations only are blessed whose God is the Lord"

A braham Lincoln knew the importance of having a right relationship with the Lord. He knew how to reason from the Bible to handle the many situations which he faced. In him we have an example of godly leadership.

> ... it is the duty of Nations as well as of men to own their dependence upon the overruling power of God, to confess their sins and transgression in humble sorrow, yet with assured hope that genuine repentance will lead to mercy and pardon, and to recognize the sublime truth announced in the Holy Scriptures and proven by all history, that "those Nations only are blessed whose God is the Lord."[19]

President Lincoln had it right. He didn't call for compromise or tolerance. He called for repentance.

It's time to remember repentance!

". . . instruments of Divine Providence"

President Lincoln, facing the dark and desperate days of the American Civil War, was able to persevere through the conflict because of his understanding of the sovereignty of God.

> I believe we are all agents and instruments of Divine Providence. I hold myself in my present position and with the authority invested in me, as an instrument of Providence. I am conscious every moment that all I am, all I have are subject to the control of a higher Power, and that Power can use me or not use me in any manner and at any time as in His wisdom might be pleasing to Him.[20]

It is humility that readies a person for God's use. We are but vessels to be used by Him.

*It's time to remember to ready
ourselves for God's use!*

". . . pray with all fervency and contrition . . ."

Prayer is not just a public show of preachers or a play to the emotional sentiments of elderly ladies. It is an act of sincere petition and humility before the Lord. Grasp the intensity of Lincoln's words as he poured out his heart as to the need for earnest prayer.

> It is fit and becoming in all people and at all times to acknowledge and revere the supreme government of God; to bow in humble submission to his chastisements; to confess and deplore their sins and transgressions, in the full conviction that "the fear of the Lord is the beginning of wisdom"; to pray with all fervency and contrition for pardon of their past offenses and for a blessing upon present and prospective action.[21]

He goes on to add:

> . . . it is peculiarly fit for us to . . . humble ourselves before Him and to pray for His mercy, to pray that we may be spared further punishment, though

most justly deserved, that our arms may be blessed and made effectual for the re-establishment of law, order, and peace, throughout the wide extent of our country, and that the inestimable boon of civil and religious liberty, earned under His guidance and blessing by the labours and suffering of our fathers, may be restored in all its original excellence.[22]

In this selection we see the heart of a President who cared deeply about the citizens he led. He humbly called them, along with himself, to acknowledge how far they had fallen from God's standard and to seek His mercy and forgiveness. Lincoln realized that this was America's only hope.

It's time to remember
to pray for God's mercy!

". . . my country has reached the point of perilous greatness . . ."

The Bible is clear on the relationship be-tween a nation's attitude toward God and its felicity. Henry W. Grady's view of the future of our Republic reflected appreciation for the truth.

> I know that my country has reached the point of perilous greatness, and that strange forces, not to be measured or comprehended, are hurrying her to heights that dazzle and blind all mortal eyes, but I know that beyond the utter-most glory is enthroned the Lord God Almighty, and that when the hour of her trial has come He will lift up His everlasting gates and bend down above her in mercy and love.[23]

America faces many perils and trials. The great Enemy of truth and liberty would snuff out her candle were it not for the grace and mercy of a loving God.

It's time to remember where our hope lies!

Nevertheless He looked upon their distress,
When He heard their cry;
And He remembered His covenant for
    their sake,
And relented according to the greatness of
    His lovingkindness.
    (Psalm 106:44-45)

Notes

[1] Noah Webster, *The American Dictionary of the English Language* (1828 facsimile edition, San Francisco: The Foundation for American Christian Education, 1967; 1995). Used by permission.

[2] Ibid.

[3] Ibid.

[4] Julian Hawthorne, ed., *Orations of American Orators* (New York: The Colonial Press, 1900), p. 4. "American Independence" by Samuel Adams. Delivered at the State House, Philadelphia, August 1, 1776.

[5] Ibid., p. 14.

[6] Ibid., p. 28. "Inaugural Address" delivered by George Washington on the occasion of his first inauguration as President of the United States on April 30, 1789 in New York City.

[7] Ibid., p. 30.

[8] Ibid., p. 54. "Inaugural Address" delivered by John Adams before both houses of Congress on assuming the presidency of the United States, March 4, 1797.

[9] Benjamin Franklin, *The Autobiography of Benjamin Franklin* (Newton, MA: Spencer Press, 1936), p. 118. The World's Greatest Literature Series.

[10] Ibid., pp. 108-109.

[11] Hawthorne, *Orations,* p. 137. "The Boston Massacre" delivered by John Hancock at Boston, March 5, 1774 after the tragic collision between British regulars and colonial dissenters occurred.

[12] James D. Richardson, *A Compilation of the Messages and Papers of the Presidents* (New York: Bureau of National

Literature, Inc., 1897), vol. I , pp. 258-259. "A Proclamation" by John Adams, 1798.

[13] Ibid., p. 259.

[14] Ibid., pp. 259-260.

[15] Ibid., p. 259. "Second Inaugural Address" by Thomas Jefferson, March 4, 1805.

[16] Ibid., vol. VII pp. 3083-3084.

[17] Charles R. Skinner, *Manual of Patriotism* (Albany, NY: Brandow Printing Company, 1900), p. 379.

[18] John Wesley Hill, *Abraham Lincoln: Man of God* (New York: G.P. Putnam's Sons, 1927), pp. 389-390.

[19] Ibid., pp. 390-391. President Lincoln responded to the Senate's call for a National Day of Prayer and Humiliation in Washington, D.C. on March 30, 1863.

[20] Hill, *Abraham Lincoln,* p. 297. The Rev. Byron Sutherland, of Washington, D.C., quotes Lincoln as saying this in reference to his contemplation of the issue of the Emancipation Proclamation in the autumn of 1862.

[21] Ibid., p. 386.

[22] Ibid., p. 387.

[23] Skinner, *Manual of Patriotism,* p. 348.

On Government

Gov'ernment, n. Direction; regulation. These precepts will serve for the government of our conduct.

1. Control; restraint. Men are apt to neglect the government of their temper and passions.

2. The exercise of authority; direction and restraint exercised over the actions of men in communities, societies or states; the administration of public affairs, according to established constitution, laws and usages, or by arbitrary edicts. Prussia rose to importance under the government of Frederick II.

3. The exercise of authority by a parent or householder. Children are often ruined by a neglect of government in parents.

Let family government be like that of our heavenly Father, mild, gentle and affectionate.

4. The system of polity in a state; that form of fundamental rules and principles by which a nation or state is governed, or by which individual

members of a body politic are to regu-
late their social actions; a constitution,
either written or unwritten, by which
the rights and duties of citizens and
public officers are prescribed and de-
fined; as a monarchical government, or
a republican government.[1]

*For unto us a child is born, unto us a son is
given: and the government shall be upon
his shoulder: . . . Of the increase of his government and peace there shall be no end.
(Isaiah 9:6-7, KJV)*

*Let every person be in subjection to the gov-
erning authorities. For there is no authority
except from God, and those which exist are
established by God. (Romans 13:1)*

*But if a man does not know how to manage
his own household, how will he take care of
the church of God? (1 Timothy 3:5)*

When asked what comes to mind upon hearing the word "government," most people will respond with such things as Washington D.C., politicians, taxes and bureaucracy. However, these are merely the external effects of something far broader and deeper.

As seen in Noah Webster's biblical definition of the word, government is first internal, then external. Government begins in the heart of the individual and moves outwardly to affect the spheres where interaction and relationships occur. The government we see at the state and national levels is actually a reflection of the spiritual condition of the people being governed.

To many Christians, government may appear to be a "necessary evil"—unrelated to the things of God. But government is one of the most emphasized themes of the Bible.

The story of man's development, as well as his understanding of the nature and character of God, is paralleled by increasing revelation about the purpose, value and framework of God-ordained government. Beginning with Adam in the Garden, we see that God placed within man the capacity for self-government. Self-government, the foundation for proper civil government, means taking responsibility for one's own actions; living according to the standard of right and wrong established universally by God.

When our first parents disobeyed God and sin entered the human race, this capability to self-govern was lost. Man became enslaved to his own appetites and will. Upon Adam's abdication to sin, Satan was only too glad to usurp his right to govern the earth. But God, in His infinite mercy and grace, had already set out a path of deliverance for humanity.

A large part of the biblical narrative contains the step-by-step restoration of godly government to man. He was tutored in the principles of righteous government as he matured in wisdom and understanding of God's ways. After the flood, God established civil government with a twofold purpose: caretaker of the rights of man and punisher of evildoers.

Eventually, God established the Hebrew theocratic republic as a pattern of proper civil government under God. Due to the internal mark of sin and humanity's proclivity toward evil, the Law could never correct the deficit in their relationship with God. There had to be another step, and "when the fulness of the time came, God sent forth His Son, born of a woman, born under the Law, in order that He might redeem those who were under the Law, that we might receive the adoption as sons" (Galatians 4:4-5).

The significance of Jesus' death and resurrection, governmentally speaking, lies in the fact that He now writes God's Law on the heart of the individual. Jesus is the new and living Way by which we gain access to the Father. With

His emphasis on the value of the individual created in the image of God, the proper alignment of governmental authority was restored.

In the centuries following the first coming of Christ, we see the causal effect of internal spiritual liberty on the external civil sphere. As the light of truth began to shine, civilization proportionally improved and prospered. The fullest expression of this connection is seen in the establishment of the world's first Christian constitutional federal republic—the United States of America. In America, we see Christian principles undergirding and permeating governmental philosophy and structure to the greatest extent that has ever been realized by the world.

In America, we see Christian principles undergirding and permeating governmental philosophy and structure to the greatest extent that has ever been realized by the world.

With all of its problems and blatant sin, America still stands as the best example of the benefits derived from building a nation upon a godly foundation. With all of its blessings, prosperity and grandeur, however, America is an infinitesimal shadow of the glory and magnificence of the kingdom that Christ will set up at His second coming. Only then will we realize the fullness of God's plan for government.

★   ★   ★

". . . neither can any Govern himselfe unless . . ."

Our founding fathers based much of our government on the wisdom of those who had gone before. Among these sages was Hugo Grotius, sixteenth-century lawyer and philosopher. He understood that the proper flow of power begins internally, then moves outward.

> He knows not how to rule a kingdome, that cannot manage a Province; nor can he wield a Province, that . . . cannot guide a Family; nor can that man Govern well a Family that knows not how to Govern himselfe; neither can any Govern himselfe unless his reason be Lord, Will and Appetite her Vassals: nor can Reason rule unlesse herselfe be ruled by God, and (wholy) be obedient to Him.[2]

Using this same biblical reasoning, our forefathers produced the great documents of America—and that reasoning is sorely needed today to preserve the Christian idea of government!

It's time to remember how to govern ourselves!

*". . . governments rather
depend upon men, than
men upon governments . . ."*

As America continues to drift further from
God's standard of morality, the adverse effects are seen in her institutions. Certainly, the
extent of government's power and intrusion has
increased dramatically in the past 100 years. William Penn, proprietor of the Pennsylvania Colony, had a biblical view of the right relationship
between the state and the individual.

> Governments, like clocks, go from the
> motions men give them; and as govern-
> ments are made and moved by men, so
> by them they are ruined too. Wherefore
> governments rather depend upon men,
> than men upon governments. . . .[3]

To some, government is like a god. It is the
source of everything necessary for a good and
prosperous life. God never intended government to supplant man's reliance upon Him.

*Its time to remember on
Whom we must depend!*

"... *avoiding* ... *to encroach upon another* ..."

The unique system of checks and balances built into our government was established with a full awareness of the depravity of man. Man instinctively gathers as much power to himself as possible. Washington warned of the consequences of one arm of the government usurping authority at another's expense.

> It is important, likewise, that the habits of thinking, in a free country, should inspire caution in those entrusted with its administration, to confine themselves within their respective constitutional spheres, avoiding, in the exercise of the powers of one department, to encroach upon another. ... [4]

The power of American courts has grown enormously. Who should really have the final say in matters of concern to our nation: the people, through their elected representatives, or the Supreme Court?

It's time to remember the importance of the separation of powers!

". . . foreign influence is one of the most baneful foes . . ."

George Washington spoke to the issue of foreign influence peddling by government officials in his Farewell Address:

> Against the insidious wiles of foreign influence (I conjure you to believe me, fellow-citizens), the jealousy of a free people ought to be constantly awake; since history and experience prove, that foreign influence is one of the most baneful foes of republican government. But that jealousy, to be useful, must be impartial; else it becomes the instrument of the very influence to be avoided, instead of a defense against it.[5]

We must hold those in power accountable to a high standard of integrity on behalf of the interests of our country. May we root out the very hint of personal and party benefit which has infiltrated our political system.

It's time to remember integrity in foreign policy!

"A man's house is his castle . . ."

The family is the first sphere of government, for it is in the family that children are taught to submit to higher authority and to relate to others. With the coming of Christianity, the biblical purpose for the family was restored along with its mandated system of self-government. Revolutionary War supporter and orator James Otis recalls the biblical concept of family sovereignty in the roots of English Common Law:

> Now one of the most essential branches of English liberty is the freedom of one's house. A man's house is his castle; whilst he is quiet, he is as well guarded as a prince in his castle.[6]

Today, the family is being assailed from within and without. Many, in the name of a good cause, violate the God-given boundary of authority that exists between the State and the family. When civil government intrudes upon the reserved rule of the family, all liberty is undermined and jeopardized.

It's time to remember the sanctity of the family!

". . . with powers properly distributed and adjusted . . ."

One purpose of government is the protection of liberty for its citizens. When the State begins to grow beyond its delegated powers, it usurps the rights of the people for its own validation. President George Washington commented about the extent and limits of government.

> And remember especially, that for the efficient management of your common interests, in a country so extensive as ours, a government of as much vigor as is consistent with the perfect security of liberty, is indispensable. Liberty itself will find in such a government, with powers properly distributed and adjusted, its surest guardian.[7]

In our clamor for security and prosperity, we must take care that we do not sell our birthright (liberty) for a pot of stew (government intervention).

*It's time to remember
the limits of government!*

"Cherish public credit"

A discussion about money must go hand-in-hand with a discussion about government. The government needs tax money to fund the protection and welfare of the community at large. President Washington exhorted frugality and accountability:

> Cherish public credit. One method of preserving it is to use it as sparingly as possible; avoiding . . . the accumulation of debt, not only by shunning occasions of expense, but by vigorous exertions in time of peace to discharge the debts which unavoidable wars may have occasioned, not ungenerously throwing upon posterity the burden we ourselves ought to bear.[8]

As the public appetite for government entitlements has grown, so has the national debt and the size of the tax burden. A biblical understanding of the limits of government and the responsibility of the individual would result in refreshing reformation in this area.

It's time to remember our fiscal responsibility!

". . . industry, wisdom, and commerce"

Samuel Adams, key figure in the establishment of the American Republic, believed in the natural vibrancy of a free economy.

> She will bring with her in her train industry, wisdom, and commerce. She thrives most when left to shoot forth in her natural luxuriance, and asks from human policy, only not to be checked in her growth by artificial encouragements.[9]

Adams believed that, left to itself with little government intervention, the free enterprise system would grow and flourish. If external pressures are placed on the system, creativity and productivity will suffer.

It's time to remember the biblical principles of economics!

". . . this . . . [is] the strongest government on earth"

America was established as a republic, not a democracy. In a constitutional republic, there is a standard of law against which representatives elected by the people test decisions. In a democracy, it is the *corporate body* which determines sovereignty. Thomas Jefferson defended the republican government in his first inaugural speech:

> I know, indeed, that some honest men fear that a republican government cannot be strong. . . . But would the honest patriot, in the full tide of successful experiment, abandon a government which has so far kept us free and firm . . . ? I trust not. I believe this, on the contrary, the strongest government on earth. . . . [10]

It is our reliance on the standard of just law, not the majority opinion, that preserves our liberty and safeguards us from tyranny.

It's time to remember the strength of our government!

"These principles form the bright constellation . . ."

President Jefferson's first inaugural speech registered the basic tenet of the republican form of government.

> Equal and exact justice to all men, of whatever state or persuasion, religious or political; peace, commerce, and honest friendship with all nations, entangling alliances with none; the support of the State governments in all their rights, as the most competent administrations for our domestic concerns, and the surest bulwarks against anti-republican tendencies . . . a well-disciplined militia, our best reliance in peace, and for the first moments of war, till the regulars may relieve them, the supremacy of the civil over the military authority; economy in the public expense, that labor may be lightly burdened, the honest payment of our debts . . . freedom of religion, freedom of the press, and freedom of the person. . . .[11]

President Jefferson concludes with a call to

vigilant watchfulness concerning the preservation of the Republic.

> These principles form the bright constellation, which has gone before us, and guided our steps through an age of revolution and reformation. The wisdom of our sages, and blood of our heroes, have been devoted to their attainment; they should be the creed of our political faith, the text of our civic instruction, the touchstone by which to try the services of those we trust; and should we wander from them in moments of error or of alarm, let us hasten to retrace our steps, and to regain the road which alone leads to peace, liberty, and safety.[12]

Popular political thought of recent years has assailed several of the key principles to which Jefferson referred. Let us beware that we not dismantle the very foundation upon which our liberty is built.

> *It's time to remember the fundamental principles of a free government!*

"This is the sum of good government . . ."

Government protecting the good of the people and staying out of their economic affairs was what Thomas Jefferson claimed to be "good government."

> Still one more thing, fellow-citizen, a wise and frugal government, which shall restrain men from injuring one another, shall leave them otherwise free to regulate their own pursuits of industry and improvement, and shall not take from the mouth of labor the bread it has earned. This is the sum of good government; and this is necessary to close the circle of our felicities.[13]

Scripture teaches that government is ordained by God to punish evildoers and praise those who do right (1 Peter 2:14). Government was not given absolute sovereignty over man. It must function within its limits to be most effective.

*It's time to remember
the biblical role of government!*

"The last hopes of mankind, therefore, rest with us . . ."

Daniel Webster captured the spirit behind the American Revolution when he noted the fundamental and manifest truth which precipitated its onset: ". . . that the powers of government are but a trust, and that they cannot be lawfully exercised but for the good of the community."[14]

Webster goes on to expound on the gravity of the American experiment.

> If, in our case, the representative system ultimately fail, popular government must be pronounced impossible. No combination of circumstances more favorable to the experiment can ever be expected to occur. The last hopes of mankind, therefore, rest with us. . . .[15]

Let us ever remember the sober responsibility we have to all of mankind in demonstrating the principles of truth and right in our Republic. "From everyone who has been given much shall much be required" (Luke 12:48).

It's time to remember
our responsibility to the world!

"Every free government is necessarily complicated . . ."

Webster taught on the value of our republican form of government. Every aspect of it was fashioned from a biblical Christian perspective.

> Every free government is necessarily complicated, because all such governments establish restraints, as well on the power of government itself as on that of individuals. If we will abolish the distinction of branches and have but one branch; if we will abolish jury trials, and leave all to the judge, we may readily simplify government. We may easily bring it to the simplest of all possible forms, a pure despotism.[16]

We are blessed in this nation to have a system of government that takes into account the depravity of man and elevates government to a nobler plane. We must diligently protect the Christian form of our government.

It's time to remember the requirements of a free government!

" . . . life, liberty, and the
pursuit of happiness . . ."

Abraham Lincoln understood the profound wisdom and far-reaching impact of the Declaration of Independence.

> "We hold these truths to be self-evident, that all men are created equal; that they are endowed by their Creator with certain unalienable rights; that among these are life, liberty, and the pursuit of happiness; that to secure these rights, governments are instituted among men, deriving their powers from the consent of the governed." There is the origin of Popular Sovereignty. Who, then, shall come in at this day, and claim that he invented it?[17]

The foundation of our liberty is the acknowledgment that man has a Creator and that his Creator has established certain principles of right and wrong.

It's time to remember
the Source of human rights!

"And what has been its history?"

At the time of the adoption of the Constitution, a heated debate raged concerning its power and potential misuse. Many wanted to cling to the weak Articles of Confederation with its loose organization and more autonomous State governments. Others saw the potential unraveling of the independence so dearly bought as factions began to emerge. Daniel Webster examined the effect of the Constitution in a speech he made several decades after its ratification.

> The Constitution of the United States, the nearest approach of mortal to perfect political wisdom, was the work of men who purchased liberty with their blood, but who found that, without organization, freedom was not a blessing. They formed it, and the people, in their intelligence adopted it. And what has been its history? Has it trodden down any man's rights? Has it circumscribed the liberty of the press? Has it stopped the mouth of any man? Has it held us up as objects of disgrace abroad? How

much the reverse! It has given us character abroad; and when, with Washington at its head, it went forth to the world, this young country at once became the most interesting and imposing in the circle of civilized nations.[18]

The fact that this document is based upon biblical principles and ratified by such a diverse group of people is testimony to the hand of God in its origin. The Constitution stands as a model of civil government for the whole world to see. Rather than allow it to be misquoted and mishandled, let us uphold its integrity with tenacious fervor!

*It's time to remember
the wisdom of our Constitution!*

". . . little power for mischief . . ."

Abraham Lincoln embraced the idea that virtuous character is important in our republican form of government. In his first inaugural address, Lincoln discussed a safeguard built into our constitutional system.

> By the frame of the government under which we live, this same people have wisely given their public servants but little power for mischief; and have, with equal wisdom, provided for the return of that little to their own hands at very short intervals. While the people retain their virtue and vigilance, no administration, by any extreme of wickedness or folly, can very seriously injure the government in the short space of four years.[19]

The concept is that the people must be vigilant to root out those who would undermine the character of our government or misuse its powers for wickedness or folly at election time.

*It's time to remember
to be discerning when we vote!*

" . . . *government of the people,*
by the people,
for the people . . . "

Abraham Lincoln's *Gettysburg Address* appears in bronze within the classic halls of Oxford (England) as a specimen of the purest English ever written or spoken.[20] It chronicles the ideals, the near demise and hopeful future of the American republic. The government of this unique nation was predicated upon biblical principles which set it as the capstone on the edifice of human experience.

> Fourscore and seven years ago our fathers brought forth on this continent, a new nation, conceived in liberty, and dedicated to the proposition that all men are created equal. . . . We here highly resolve that these dead shall not have died in vain, that this nation under God shall have a new birth of freedom, and that government of the people, by the people, for the people, shall not perish from the earth.[21]

The phrase "government of the people, by the people, for the people" had been used numerous times prior to Lincoln by such orators as Daniel Webster, James Douglas, James Porter and Theodore Parker. Its first presentation apparently was in the preface to the old Wycliffe Bible, translated in 1382. It was there declared, "This Bible is for the government of the people by the people and for the people."[22] The seeds of the Protestant Reformation bore great fruit in the founding of the American republic nearly 400 years later. May we continue to harvest the fruit from our biblical beginnings.

It's time to remember
our unique heritage as a nation!

"Let reverence of the law . . . become the political religion of the Nation"

President Lincoln's respect for the law is seen in this passage:

> Let reverence of the law be breathed by every mother to the lisping babe that prattles on her lap; let it be taught in schools, seminaries, and colleges; let it be written in the primers, spelling-books, and almanacs; let it be preached from the pulpits, and proclaimed in the legislative halls, and enforced in the halls of justice; in short, let it become the political religion of the Nation.[23]

It is the law that forms the foundation for right government. If this law is based upon the Word of God, which is the case in the American republic, and the people choose to obey it, the nation will be blessed.

It's time to remember the sanctity of just laws!

"There is higher sanction . . ."

Constitutions do not make people; people make constitutions. Our constitution is great and admirable, because the men who made it were so and the people who ratified it and have lived under it were brave, intelligent, and lovers of liberty. There is a higher sanction and a surer protection to life and liberty, to the right of free speech and trial by jury, to justice and humanity, in the traditions, the beliefs, the habits of mind, and the character of the American people than any which can be afforded by any constitution, no matter how wisely drawn.

—Henry Cabot Lodge[24]

Right government begins in the heart of the individual. The Constitution, marvelous document that it is, is only the external effect of a people who reasoned from the Bible to the civil political sphere.

*It's time to remember
the standard for government!*

". . . no nation founded upon injustice can stand"

The phrase from our Pledge of Allegiance proclaims, "with liberty and justice for all." These are not just nice-sounding words. They are the very heart of the Christian principles embodied in our Constitution. Roger G. Ingersoll nicely summarizes this sentiment.

> A government founded upon anything except liberty and justice cannot and ought not to stand. All the wrecks on either side of the stream of time, all the wrecks of the great cities, and all the nations that have passed away—all are a warning that no nation founded upon injustice can stand.[25]

The principles of justice and equality are Christian principles. If we turn our backs on Christianity, we will lose its blessings and its protection.

*It's time to remember
justice and equality, America!*

"Do you remember . . .?"

Have you ever thought what the government has cost? Do you realize what free government means? Do you remember, as you have read the story of ages gone, how the barons met at Runnymede? Do you remember how they wrested a charter from the king? Do you remember how the Ironsides went into battle? Do you remember the psalm that rang out at the shock of the conflict? Do you remember Feneuil Hall, and Massachusetts, and John Hancock? Do you remember Carpenter's Hall and Benjamin Franklin? Do you remember Virginia and George Washington? Do you remember what the liberty we have has cost, and are you willing to let the Republic get into the rapids simply because there are not strong enough men straining at the oars and keeping us back in the midstream of safety?

—Stewart L. Woodford[26]

Where are the valiant men and women of our generation who are willing to participate in restoring our Christian foundation as a nation? There is still hope that this grand republic can carry on, but it will take men and women of conviction and courage to humble themselves, pray for America, and then become active in restoring a biblical standard to business, education, government and family life.

It's time to act, America!

> *And I searched for a man among them who should build up the wall and stand in the gap before Me for the land, that I should not destroy it. . . . (Ezekiel 22:30)*

Notes

[1] Noah Webster, *The American Dictionary of the English Language* (1828 facsimile edition, San Francisco: The Foundation for American Christian Education, 1967; 1995). Used by permission.

[2] Rosalie J. Slater, *Teaching and Learning America's Christian History: The Principle Approach* (San Francisco: The Foundation for American Christian Education, 1965; 1993), p. 119. Used by permission.

[3] Ibid., p. 203. Cited from William Penn's *Frame of Government of Pennsylvania*, 1682.

[4] Julian Hawthorne, ed., *Orations of American Orators* (New York: The Colonial Press, 1900), p. 40, "Farewell Address."

[5] Ibid., p. 43.

[6] Ibid., p. 23, "On the Writs of Assistance" by James Otis. Delivered before the Supreme Court of Massachusetts, during the term held at Boston, in February 1761.

[7] Ibid., p. 38, "Farewell Address."

[8] Ibid., p. 41.

[9] Ibid., p. 15, "American Independence" by Samuel Adams. Delivered at the State House, Philadelphia, August 1, 1776.

[10] Ibid., pp. 142-143, "Inaugural Address" delivered by Thomas Jefferson at the commencement of his first term as President of the Unites States on March 4, 1801.

[11] Ibid., pp. 143-144.

[12] Ibid., pp. 142-143.

[13] Ibid., pp. 143.

[14] Horace E. Henderson, ed., *The Academy Classics* (New York: Allyn and Bacon, 1923), p. 51. From "Webster's First Bunker Hill Oration" on the fiftieth anniversary of the Battle of Bunker Hill, June 17, 1825.

[15] Ibid., p. 56.

[16] Charles R. Skinner, *Manual of Patriotism* (Albany, NY: Brandow Printing Company, 1900), p. 353.

[17] Ibid., p. 351.

[18] Ibid., p. 354.

[19] Philip Van Doren Stern, *The Life and Writings of Abraham Lincoln* (New York: The Modern Library, Random House, Inc., 1942), p. 656. "First Inaugural Address" by Abraham Lincoln, March 4, 1861.

[20] John Wesley Hill, *Abraham Lincoln: Man of God* (New York: G.P. Putnam's Sons, 1927), p. 268.

[21] Ibid., pp. 271-272.

[22] Ibid., pp. 269-270.

[23] Skinner, *Manual of Patriotism*, p. 372.

[24] Ibid. From a speech on the adoption of the Spanish-American Treaty, United States Senate, January 24, 1899.

[25] Ibid., p. 355.

[26] Ibid., p. 369.

On Union and Unity

U'nion, n. [L. *unio,* to unite, from unus, one]
1. The act of joining two or more things into one, and thus forming a compound body or a mixture; or the junction or coalition of things thus united. Union differs from connection, as it implies the bodies to be in contact, without an intervening body; whereas things may be connected by the intervention of a third body, as by a cord or chain.
One kingdom, joy and union without end.
2. Concord; agreement and conjunction of mind, will, affections or interest. Happy is the family where perfect union subsists between all its members. . . .
7. States united. Thus the United States of America are sometimes called the Union.[1]

U'nity, n. [L. *unitas*]

1. The state of being one; oneness. Unity may consist of a simple substance or existing being, as the soul; but usually it consists in a close junction of particles or parts, constituting a body detached from other bodies. Unity is a thing undivided itself, but separate from every other thing. . . .

4. In Christian theology, oneness of sentiment, affection or behavior.

How good and how pleasant it is for brethren to dwell together in unity! Ps. 133.

Unity of faith, is an equal belief of the same truths of God, and possession of the grace of faith in like form and degree.

Unity of spirit, is the oneness which subsists between Christ and his saints, by which the same spirit dwells in both, and both have the same disposition and aims; and it is the oneness of Christians among themselves, united under the same head, having the same spirit dwelling in them, and possessing the same graces, faith, love, hope, &c.[2]

Behold, how good and how pleasant it is
For brothers to dwell together in unity! . . .
For there the LORD *commanded the bless-*
     ing—life forever. (Psalm 133:1, 3)

. . . make my joy complete by being of the
same mind, maintaining the same love,
united in spirit, intent on one purpose.
(Philippians 2:2)

. . . with all humility and gentleness, with
patience, showing forbearance to one an-
other in love, being diligent to preserve the
unity of the Spirit in the bond of peace.
(Ephesians 4:2-3)

Till we all come in the unity of the faith,
and of the knowledge of the Son of God,
unto a perfect man, unto the measure of the
stature of the fulness of Christ . . . (Ephe-
sians 4:13, KJV)

Individuality, unity and union are closely linked in the Bible. Jesus taught that the greatest commandment is for us to love God with all our being. This is the beginning point of all that matters about life and existence. He went on to say that the second greatest commandment is to love our neighbor as ourselves.

From this lesson, we see that only when we, as individuals, have a proper relationship with the Father will we relate fully and appropriately to our fellow human beings. It is the first, or vertical, relationship with God, that furnishes success in the second, or horizontal, relationship with our neighbors.

This duality of being—the individual relating to a higher authority, while at the same time relating corporately to his peers—is reflected in our federal republic. Each citizen is a citizen of the United States of America while at the same time a citizen of a state; each state is a member of the United States and at the same time there exists a coequal horizontal relationship to the other forty-nine states that make up the union called the United States of America.

Only when a state, or an individual, relates properly to the Sovereign can consent be given to walk in unity with the other parties in association. The resulting union is strong and dynamic and cannot easily be broken. The idea of voluntary consent is essential in understanding the biblical principle of union with unity.[3]

This principle of union with unity that hall-
marks the United States of America has its roots
in the Pilgrims who, according to William Brad-
ford in his history of Ply-
mouth   Plantation,
"shook off this yoke of
anti-Christian bondage,
and as ye Lords free
people, joyned them
selves (by a covenant of
the Lord into a church
estate), in ye felowship
of ye gospell, to walke in
all his wayes...."[4]

*Only when a state,
or an individual,
relates properly to
the Sovereign can
consent be given to
walk in unity with
the other parties
in association.*

As the American colonies grew and developed, each had its own unique expression of
individuality. One way to readily observe this
is to note the forms of church government
each tended to embrace. This rich diversity
did not divide or isolate the colonists, but provided a framework for appreciating the rights
of every man to self-determine in matters of
conscience.

In truth, there was a common thread which
related the colonies on a deeper level. They
fully embraced the foundational precepts of
Christianity and the decisive authority of the
Bible. For 150 years prior to the war they had
practiced Christian self-government. They understood that their rights were given by God,
not man. This belief united them in principle
and in spirit. The stage was set for their amal-

gamation into "one body politic" on a larger scale than the Pilgrims could have realized.

The twenty years leading up to the War for Independence were marked with intense education, lobbying and solicitation by men like Samuel Adams, whose Committees of Correspondence gave impetus to the rallying cry for union and independence. Without this unity of cause and spirit, there could never have been a Declaration of Independence. England would have snuffed out the spark of liberty before it could have been fanned into flame.

It was the Declaration and the war that united the colonies externally. The ratification of the Constitution then sealed the internal unity and external union into the world's first Christian constitutional federal republic. Seventeen hundred years of Christianity were culminated in this great experiment in government by the people under the law of God.

Today, America faces a great threat to her unity and ultimately to her union. The threat is not unlike that which divided the nation asunder during the Civil War. The Bible tells us that what begins in the heart, eventually makes its way into the external realm. Pressures from within and without strain the Union. Multiculturalism, with its emphasis on maintaining individual cultures at the expense of developing a cohesive national culture, chips away at the Judeo-Christian ethic that initially provided a common cord of

American philosophy and experience. Special rights protecting homosexuality and radical feminism continue to undermine the once secure foundation of our Republic. As competing factions seek self-preservation and aggrandizement at any cost, our American Republic is undermined. The America of history appears, at times, to be teetering on the brink of inward collapse.

The only hope for healing the widening rifts between races, nationalities and various worldviews is to return to the "exalted virtues of the Christian system." Through Christ, barriers are broken down and bridges are built. No one people group is exempt from the call to repentance. But as Christians, we must take the lead. We must forgive past offenses and mark out a new course where our brotherhood under one Lord is accepted and promoted. The phrase *"E Pluribus Unum"* is stamped on our coins. It means "one from the many." That is our strength and our destiny. May God help us attain it.

★   ★   ★

"... the immense value of your national union ..."

George Washington understood the biblical principle of unity. He realized that in order for this nation to endure, the people must cherish that which binds them together and guard against anything that would separate them into jealous and selfish factions.

> The unity of government which constitutes you one people is now also dear to you. It is justly so, for it is a main pillar in the edifice of your real independence, the support of your real tranquillity at home, your peace abroad, of your safety, of your prosperity, of that very liberty which you so highly prize. But as it is easy to foresee, that from different causes and from different quarters, much pains will be taken, many artifices employed, to weaken in your minds the conviction of this truth; as this is the point in your political fortress against which the batteries of internal and external enemies will be most constantly and actively (though often covertly and insidiously)

directed, it is of infinite moment that you should properly estimate the immense value of your national union, to your collective and individual happiness. . . .[5]

He continues with reference to the unity that supports all they hold dear:

. . . that you should cherish a cordial, habitual, and immovable attachment to it; accustoming yourselves to think and speak of it as of the palladium of your political safety and prosperity, watching for its preservation with jealous anxiety; discountenancing whatever may suggest even a suspicion that it can in any event be abandoned; and indignantly frowning upon the first dawning of every attempt to alienate any portion of our country from the rest, or to enfeeble the sacred ties which now link together the various parts.[6]

Appreciating and valuing one's heritage is good and desirable, but not when it causes ethnocentrism, isolationism and the growth of factions. Let us promote unity with diversity as a way of preserving our union.

It's time to remember the importance of unity!

". . . a main prop
of your liberty . . ."

Washington viewed the citizens of the newly formed nation as one people with differences considered only minor when compared to the ties that bound them together.

> Citizen, by birth or choice, of a common country, that country has a right to concentrate your affections. The name of American, which belongs to you in your national capacity, must always exalt the just pride of patriotism more than any appellation derived from local discriminations. With slight shades of difference, you have the same religion, manners, habits, and political principles. You have, in a common cause, fought and triumphed together; the independence and liberty you possess are the work of joint councils and joint efforts, of common dangers, sufferings, and successes.[7]

> In this sense it is that your union ought to be considered as a main prop of your liberty, and that the love of the

one ought to endear to you the preservation of the other.

These considerations speak a persuasive language to every reflecting and virtuous mind, and exhibit the continuance of the union as a primary object of patriotic desire. . . . With such powerful and obvious motives to union, affecting all parts of our country, while experience shall not have demonstrated its impracticability, there will always be reason to distrust the patriotism of those who, in any quarter, may endeavor to weaken its bands.[8]

The assault on the unity of our nation is escalating with fierce fervor. Let us scrutinize the motive of any who would dissuade us from wholly embracing our national identity as, first and foremost, Americans.

It's time to remember
what joins us together as a nation!

"It opens the door to foreign influence and corruption . . ."

Washington further warns that the excesses of party allegiance may result in the demise of the government as a whole. Sadly, one does not have to look very far to see the effect of political positioning and posturing in America today. Time will tell whether our nation's foreign policy has been manipulated by those who seek power and reward at the expense of the public good.

> The alternate domination of one faction over another, sharpened by the spirit of revenge . . . is itself a frightful despotism. But this leads at length to a more formal and permanent despotism. The disorders and miseries, which result, gradually incline the minds of men to seek security and repose in the absolute power of an individual; and sooner or later, the chief of some prevailing faction, more able and more fortunate than his competitors, turns this disposition to the purposes of his own elevation on the ruins of public liberty. . . .

. . . It serves to always distract the public councils, and enfeeble the public administration. It agitates the community with ill-founded jealousies and false alarms; kindles the animosity of one part against another; foments occasionally riot and insurrection. It opens the door to foreign influence and corruption, which find a facilitated access to the government itself, through the channels of party passion. The policy and will of one country are subjected to the policy and will of another.[9]

Far more important than the narrow concerns of a political party or a special interest group is the fact that we are Americans working for the good of all.

It's time to remember that political factions can destroy unity!

"... to sacrifice their individual advantages ..."

President Washington schooled the nation in what he saw as four essentials to the well-being of the United States. His final point concerns the principle of union.

> ... The prevalence of that pacific and friendly disposition among the people of the United States which will induce them to forget their local prejudices and politics; to make those mutual concessions which are requisite to the general prosperity; and, in some instances, to sacrifice their individual advantages to the interest of the community.[10]

In this brief treatise, Washington outlines the Christian character necessary for the preservation of our republic. Faction, selfishness and greed must be replaced by brotherhood and personal sacrifice.

It's time to remember
the need for selfless service!

"... a copious fountain of national, social, and personal happiness"

Orator and statesman Daniel Webster declared the virtues of our union to be a
great source of national pride.

> That Union we reached only by the dis-
> cipline of our virtue in the severe school
> of adversity.... And although our coun-
> try has stretched out, wider and wider,
> and our population spread farther and
> farther, they have not outrun its protec-
> tion or its benefits. It has been to us all a
> copious fountain of national, social, and
> personal happiness.[11]

Union with unity brings with it very practical
benefits. The disruption to our economy and
our security would be immense should our
unity be broken. The great diversity of America
need not be a hindrance to her union. It should
be her greatest asset.

*It's time to remember
the blessings of dwelling in unity!*

" . . . let the Bible be
. . . on the same shelf
with the Constitution . . ."

Robert C. Winthrop, descendant of Massachusetts Bay Colony founder John Winthrop and legislator in the mid-1800s, was an
outspoken advocate of the importance of the
Bible and religion in the health and welfare of
the nation.

> Let the Banner of the Cross go forth
> side by side with the Flag of our Union
> wherever it is carried; let the Spirit of
> the Lord be invoked to accompany the
> Spirit of Liberty in its triumphant
> march; let the Bible be everywhere on
> the same shelf with the Constitution;
> let there be no region so remote, no
> valley so secluded, no wilderness so
> solitary or so desolate, that men shall
> be able to escape from the visible pres-
> ence of Religion, as manifested in the
> observance of the Lord's Day, and in
> that most attractive and fascinating of
> all its forms, —the religious instruction
> of young children; let this be accom-
> plished, and, depend on it, the people

of this country will have much the less
to fear for the stability of their institutions, and Congresses and Cabinets
will have much less to do to preserve
the Union. There will then, too, be no
longer any doubt that we are a "power
on earth"; a power for every purpose
of promoting either the welfare of
men, or the glory of God.[12]

What a marvelous commentary on the role of
Christianity in supporting and maintaining the
integrity of our union. There is so much to gain
from ordering our society upon God's principles for living and relating. The Bible is the perfect vehicle for uniting us as one nation under
God.

It's time to remember
the Christian roots of our Union!

"We are not enemies, but friends"

At the outset of his first term, President Abraham Lincoln faced the huge challenge of holding together a Union whose passions were a powder keg. He appealed to their history and character as a people to prevail in preserving their unity.

> We are not enemies, but friends. We must not be enemies. Though passion may have strained, it must not break our bonds of affection. The mystic chords of memory, stretching from every battlefield and patriot grave to every living heart and hearth-stone all over this broad land, will yet swell the chorus of the Union when again touched, as surely they will be, by the better angels of our nature.[13]

The sword of division struck the very heart of the nation. Let us concentrate on what binds us together, remembering the challenges we have faced as a nation.

It's time to remember the lessons of history!

"Liberty is your birthright . . ."

Justice and liberty are for all in a Christian republic. Abraham Lincoln had to deal with the curse of slavery that had overshadowed our land. He spoke of liberty, its Author and its responsibilities to a group of emancipated slaves.

> My poor friends, you are free; free as the air [he said], you can cast off the name of slave and trample on it. It will come to you no more. Liberty is your birthright; God gave it to you as he gave it to others and it is a sin that you have been deprived of it for so many years. But, you must try to deserve this priceless boon. Let the world see that you merit it and are able to maintain it by your good works. Don't let your joy carry you into excesses. Learn the laws and obey them. Obey God's commandments and thank Him for giving you liberty for it is to Him that you owe all things.[14]

It's time to remember
the responsibility of freedom!

"One God, one country, one destiny"

Were it not for the intense love of country that existed before and after the War Between the States, this nation would have ceased to exist as it had been formed. From the earliest days of the Republic, men expressed a deep sense of loyalty and devotion to the union that formed these United States. Here is a sampling of their sentiments:

> The kindred blood that flows in the veins of American citizens, the mingled blood which they have shed in defense of their sacred rights, consecrate their Union.
>
> —James Madison

> One God, one country, one destiny. This is the gospel of American nationality.
>
> —Wendell Phillips

> I know no North, no South, no East, no West to which I owe any allegiance.
>
> —Henry Clay

Every American should be proud of his
whole country, rather than a part.
>—William Tecumseh Sherman

Without Union our independence and
liberty would never have been
achieved; without Union they cannot
be maintained.
>—Andrew Jackson

We are One by the configuration of nature and by the strong impress of the
art. We are One by the memories of
our fathers. We are One by the hopes
of our children. We are one by our
Constitution and our Union.
>—Robert C. Winthrop

The nation depends not on the wisdom
of its senators, not on the vigilance of
its police, not on the strong arm of its
standing armies: but on the loyalty of a
united people.
>—Parke Godwin [15]

Lord of the Universe! Shield us and
   guide us,
Trusting Thee always, through shad-
   ows and sun!
Thou hast united us, who shall divide
   us?
Keep us, O keep us, the MANY IN
   ONE.
>—Oliver Wendell Holmes[16]

*Finally, brethren, rejoice, be made complete,
be comforted, be like-minded, live in peace;
and the God of love and peace shall be with
you. (2 Corinthians 13:11)*

Notes

[1] Noah Webster, *The American Dictionary of the English Language* (1828 facsimile edition, San Francisco: The Foundation for American Christian Education, 1967; 1995). Used by permission.

[2] Ibid.

[3] Verna Hall and Rosalie Slater have identified seven biblical principles of government upon which the American founding documents are based. The seventh principle is called the Christian Principle of American Political Union. For an in-depth study of the Principle Approach to American Christian Education and the seven biblical principles of government, contact the Foundation for American Christian Education in Chesapeake, VA.

[4] Rosalie J. Slater, *Teaching and Learning America's Christian History: The Principle Approach* (San Francisco: Foundation for American Christian Education, 1965; 1993), p. 267. Used by permission.

[5] Julian Hawthorne, ed., *Orations of American Orators.* (New York: The Colonial Press, 1900), pp. 33-34. "Farewell Address" delivered by George Washington on the occasion of his departure from the second term of his presidency. Published on September 17, 1796.

[6] Ibid.

[7] Ibid., p. 34.

[8] Ibid., p. 35.

[9] Ibid., pp. 35-36.

[10] Ibid., pp. 38-39.

[11] Charles R. Skinner, *Manual of Patriotism* (Albany, NY: Brandow Printing Company, 1900), p. 359.

[12] Verna M. Hall, *The Christian History of the American Revolution: Consider and Ponder* (San Francisco: Foundation for American Christian Education, 1976), p. 21. From a speech given on the Anniversary Meeting of the American Sunday School Union in Boston, May 27, 1852. Used by permission.

[13] Philip Van Doren Stern, *The Life and Writings of Abraham Lincoln* (New York: The Modern Library, Random House, Inc., 1942), p. 657. "First Inaugural Address" by Abraham Lincoln, March 4, 1861.

[14] John Wesley Hill, *Abraham Lincoln: Man of God* (New York: G.P. Putnam's Sons, 1927), pp. 416-417.

[15] Skinner, *Manual of Patriotism,* pp. 377-380. Includes quotes from Madison, Phillips, Clay, Sherman, Jackson, Winthrop and Godwin.

[16] Skinner, *Manual of Patriotism*, p. 365.

Why Use the 1828 Dictionary?

Words are of paramount importance. They convey the very thoughts and intentions of man's heart. According to the Bible, words have great power: They bring either life or death. Improper use of words results in imperfect understanding of ideas. The language of a nation is one of its defining points, a hallmark of its individuality. "A national language is a band of national union," wrote Noah Webster in 1789, the year the United States Constitution was ratified.[1] It was this idea that compelled Noah Webster painstakingly, over a period of more than twenty years, to research and record in his own hand the language of the American people.

Hence, in the year A.D. 1828, Noah Webster published his *American Dictionary of the English Language*. To Webster this was a vitally needed resource for the young United States of America. Webster held strongly the view that in order for America to grow and prosper, she had to cut the ties with England and the rest of

Europe. He was persuaded that it is through its language that a nation most explicitly establishes its identity. Webster's dictionary surpassed the highly respected dictionary of Samuel Johnson by adding 12,000 words.

Many of the new words that Webster included were directly related to the emerging American philosophy of government with its Christian foundation. Webster's definitions resulted from his intensive research of the Holy Scriptures, as well as analysis of the twenty-six foreign languages he mastered. They reflect a biblical worldview as well as an understanding of the principles of Christian constitutional government.

The 1828 dictionary is replete with scriptural references to bring greater illumination to the meanings of words. In essence, Webster's dictionary was a tutorial for the citizenry in the precepts of biblical reasoning and its application to the republican form of government.[2]

This was not the only thing that set the 1828 dictionary apart. Noah Webster believed that there was a proper and efficient order in which word meanings should appear in a definition. After exhaustive etymological research, Webster identified the primary sense, or idea, of the word. It was this essence of original meaning that was placed first, before all other uses. Webster was liberated from simply using common synonyms as substitute definitions for words. He traced the root meanings of words from their sources to the various current expressions.[3]

Finally, Webster established a standard of purity for the language by expunging many of the cant, vulgar and obscene words that had been incorporated into other English dictionaries at that time. If language represents the views and values of a nation, it must transcend the petty and the vain, the corrupted and devalued vocabulary that accompanies the faddish and transitory philosophy of a given generation. Webster did acknowledge that a language is living. It grows as new ideas and concepts are discovered through the introduction of new arts and, in particular, new ideas in the sciences. He held firmly, though, that the underlying chief impetus of the language must be retained at all cost.[4]

One might still ask, "Why define words today using a dictionary that was written more than 175 years ago? After all, is ours not a living language, fluid and evolving from year to year?" That is precisely the point of using *the* dictionary that was *the* definitive work at the time when our national identity was being established. It is true enough that a language will grow and mature. Some meanings of words may shift in emphasis and importance; some words may fall out of use altogether.

Not all growth, however, is positive, to be sure. Over time, the meanings, spellings and pronunciations can be corrupted. That is to say that they drift from their original intent to something of a watered-down, colloquial or modish meaning. When this is the case, it is difficult to comprehend fully what was intended in the writings of the great statesmen and authors of bygone days. To completely appreciate what our founding fathers believed, it is necessary for us to understand the meanings of the words they used as they used them, not as we might popularly use them today.

In the writing of this book, Webster's 1828 dictionary is used to define each of the chapter titles. The intent of such a selection is to enable the reader to understand the subjects in the same light that the founders would have understood them. It is most necessary, especially in an age characterized by politically correct prattle rather than substantive discourse, to re-define terms in light of their fundamental and historical meanings. As stated before, if we want to gain insight into the wisdom of our ancestors, we must understand their words as they used and meant them.

Educator and historian Rosalie J. Slater examines the life and contributions of Noah Webster in her treatise that appears in the Foundation for American Christian Education's facsimile edition of the *American Dictionary of the English Language* (1828). Miss Slater cites Webster's original dictionary as a valuable tool for us today because "it remains a repository of three essential ingredients of *America's Christian His-*

tory. It reflects our Christian philosophy of life, our Christian philosophy of government, and our Christian philosophy of education."[5] She goes on to say,

> Unmistakably it reveals the degree to which the Bible was America's basic textbook and how it is related to all fields. Noah Webster as a Christian scholar laid his foundation of etymology upon the Scriptures and his research into the origin of language stems from this premise. One cannot read his definitions nor study his discussion of the grammatical construction of our language without encountering at every point a scriptural Christian philosophy of life.[6]

What may be viewed by many as a curious, if not obsolete, relic from the past is in actuality a marvelous reservoir of Christian truth and reasoning from which to draw in order to renovate our own age. Amazingly, Webster's 1828 *American Dictionary of the English Language* continues to influence America today. The F.A.C.E. facsimile edition and a recent CD-ROM version are appearing across the nation and around the world in homes, Christian schools, churches, Bible studies—wherever people are seeking biblical truth.

The biblical pattern for education was first

established in Old Testament times and continued through the years of the early Church. We see it fully flower during the colonial and founding periods of our nation. God's Word never changes, nor does it lose its power to affect all who hear and abide by its teachings. This same approach that produced so much of value in the past and preserved it for us can do likewise in our world today and for our posterity.

Notes

[1] Noah Webster, *The American Dictionary of the English Language* (1828 facsimile edition, San Francisco: The Foundation for American Christian Education, 1967; 1995) in the Preface: "Noah Webster: Founding Father of American Scholarship and Education," by Rosalie J. Slater, p. 26. Used by permission.

[2] Ibid., p. 24.

[3] Ibid.

[4] Ibid., p. 25.

[5] Ibid.

[6] Ibid.

Key Individuals in America's Christian History

It is indisputable that God works through individuals and nations alike. The Bible is full of stories that validate both aspects of this statement. Every generation has its share of men and women who stand tall among their peers—some for good, some for evil. Nothing makes the study of history more meaningful, more inspiring and more alive than to get to know the people who shaped the world in which we live as they laughed and labored, wept and wrote, dreamed and dared.

A sad development of our own time is the denigration of the role models of the past. Popular thinking demands the leveling of all that is good and honorable and ennobled. There seems to be a conspiracy of mediocrity which exacts a heavy toll on any who are held in high esteem. Certainly every individual has his failures and shortcomings, and we must take care not to elevate anyone beyond propriety. There are, however, certain values and qualities that are extremely important in any culture and are best demonstrated, taught and preserved through the heroic examples of those who have "fought the good fight" in preceding generations.

We draw strength, hope and even faith through examining the lives of those who were obedient to the purposes of God in their time. They stand as beacon lights to guide the inexperienced and novice to a secure and safe landing along the shores of contemporary life. It is with this in mind that these brief profiles of some of the people whose words are recorded in this book are here included. The reader is encouraged to do a thorough study of these men using their own writings and other primary sources.

Jesus, the Christ

Jesus stands as the greatest role model of all time for all time. In Him, we see a perfect picture of our Heavenly Father (John 14:9). His wisdom is unapproachable (Romans 11:33), His example of servant-leadership unsurpassed (Matthew 20:22). He stands as the focal point of all history and time. Jesus Christ is the standard against which all that is noble and just and wise and good must be measured. There is no one who approaches Him in perfection and completeness.

John Quincy Adams (1767-1848)

A bright star in the Adams constellation, John Quincy was a boy-statesman who later became president. Adams was groomed for public service by his father, the passionate Puritan John Adams. He was prepared for the art of living by his mother, Abigail, who reared him alone during the father's frequent absences.

At the age of twelve, John Q. traveled with his father to Europe and thus began a career of public service. His servant-leadership is best exemplified in his return to Congress after a failed bid for a second term in the presidency. During these last eighteen years of his life, Adams made significant contributions, among them a relentless call for the abolition of slavery. John Quincy Adams embraced the tenets of orthodox Christianity with a passion. They were the guiding lights of his life and the anchor to which all his reasoning was moored. Adams died on the floor of the House at age eighty-one, still putting to use his lifelong gift of service.

Samuel Adams (1722-1803)

Called the "Father of the American Revolution," Sam Adams was a fiery individual with a passion for liberty. Adams entered Harvard with the intent of becoming a clergyman, but chose a career in politics instead. It was Sam Adams' brilliant concept of the Committees of Correspondence that educated and united the widely diverse American colonies. It was his tenacious call for independence that helped mold the consensus toward the Declaration of 1776.

With his name firmly affixed on that document, Adams laid his life on the line for the cause for which he had so fervently fought. Not particularly eloquent of speech, Adams nevertheless commanded much respect for his tenacious pursuit of liberty and justice. Samuel Adams was a devout Christian. He recognized the importance of laying the foundation for the new nation on the principles of Christianity and in passing the Truth on to posterity.

Benjamin Franklin (1706-1790)

As a lad, Ben Franklin moved to Philadelphia where he was apprenticed to his brother, a printer. This was the providential beginning of a man who greatly influenced the founding of this nation. Sometimes pictured as a man of scurrilous character, Franklin's own writings defend his reputation and character. He is frequently claimed to be a Deist by those seeking to undermine the Christian nature of the founding of America.

It should be noted that Franklin never publicly professed a belief in the divinity of Jesus; in fact, he openly questioned it. He did, however, believe in the value and importance of the principles of Christianity for the success of the nation. Franklin firmly held that God rules in the affairs of men and that He will reward each man in the next life according to how he lived on earth—not at all what a Deist would say or believe. Benjamin Franklin contributed much in the area of science, diplomacy and journalism, but it was his wit and wisdom that won the hearts of his countrymen and secured a place for him among America's founding fathers.

John Hancock (1737-1793)

The emboldened and oversized signature of John Hancock on the Declaration of Independence stands as a symbol of his courage and strength of character. Born to wealth, Hancock eschewed the safety and security of the Tories, who remained loyal to the English Crown. He was a man of polished manners, charitable and public-spirited. He willingly gave of his own resources to help fund the great efforts of the colonists to break free from British tyranny.

It was the British expedition sent out to capture Hancock and his colleague, Sam Adams, that precipitated the battle of Lexington, marking the onset of the War for Independence. John Hancock went on to become the governor of Massachusetts for repeated terms until his death. He stands tall among those whose lives and fortunes were laid on the line for the cause of liberty.

Patrick Henry (1736-1799)

Perhaps the greatest American orator of all time, Patrick Henry was an unlikely candidate for such an accolade—at least on the surface. Henry squandered his youth in idle activity and meandering, achieving little in his schooling. As a young man he became a lawyer, realizing little success at first. Remarkably, something was awakened within him that set him on the course for which the Lord had intended him. As Henry gave impassioned pleas on behalf of his clients, no jury could remain unaffected.

His fame spread throughout the colony. He intuitively knew how to touch the hearts of men with a passion of fire. It was this quality that opened the door for service in the Virginia House of Burgesses and, eventually, in the governorship. Henry was a devout Christian who made no apologies for the religious nature and Christian underpinnings of the fledgling nation he helped found. God greatly used Patrick Henry to call forth liberty and then to set a watchful eye upon its progress.

Thomas Jefferson (1743-1826)

In many ways Thomas Jefferson has been an enigma among historians. He burst upon the colonial scene at a time when the debate concerning independence was already heated. It was his great abilities with the pen that secured him the commission to draft the Declaration of Independence. While not solely the work of Jefferson, the final document is yet to be rivaled among the political works of man.

During the years that Jefferson was most involved in government and his ideas most influential, he held to orthodox Christian beliefs. Whether he ever accepted the divinity of Christ is frequently debated. It is no secret that Jefferson abhorred the trappings and embellishments imposed upon Christianity by pompous and power-hungry men. It was these external aspects of organized religion that he rejected soundly.

The true principles of Christianity, however, were highly revered by Jefferson. In fact, it was President Jefferson who sent missionaries armed with Bibles to educate the Indians in the western parts of the expanding country. It appears that as Jefferson grew older, he came increasingly under the influence of the European Enlightenment and may have strayed from his earlier commitment to orthodoxy. By this time, Jefferson had retired to his home, Monticello, where he spent the remainder of his days in correspondence and scientific inquiry. He was truly a genius of great proportions and used strategically by God in the founding of our nation.

Abraham Lincoln (1809-1865)

Descendant of a Pennsylvania Quaker family, Abraham Lincoln was born a pioneer in Kentucky. With little formal education, Lincoln's own strength of character and aspirations left an indelible mark on the pages of American history. Lincoln was a folksy person with an incredible way of speaking to the heart of issues honestly and sincerely.

Attracted to the field of law, Lincoln was catapulted onto the political stage as a foe to slavery in the Lincoln-Douglas debate. Not long after, the new Republican Party nominated him as its choice for the presidency. That God had prepared Lincoln for the darkest hour of America's story can be most readily seen in his Gettysburg Address, which stands among the world's most eloquent and concise examples of literary expression.

Lincoln's relationship with the Lord matured as he did, eventually culminating in his acknowledgment of his need for the Savior of mankind. Lincoln's strength of conviction and down-to-earth wisdom continue to touch the hearts of all who seek true liberty.

James Otis (1725-1783)

As a member of the New England aristocracy, James Otis could have hidden behind the security of his wealth and name, remaining loyal to Great Britain. This, however, was not the kind of man Otis was. In actuality, he was among the very first to step forth and protest loudly and effectively the atrocities the colonists endured at the hands of their overlords. Otis was the recipient of a liberal Bostonian education. He drew from its richness in the classics and history in defending human rights. Otis greatly influenced the public debate which evolved into the War for Independence.

Otis's large stature and booming voice—not to mention his generous funding of the war effort from his own resources—made him one of the most sought-after men by the British authorities. James Otis lost his life in a tragic accident which kept him from seeing the full realization of the ideals for which he tirelessly fought. The legacy he left, however, brought forth great fruit in the world's first Christian constitutional republic.

George Washington (1732-1799)

"First in war, first in peace, and first in the hearts of his countrymen." Thus was the beloved "Father of our Country" eulogized by Henry Lee upon his death. Large of physical stature and presence, the greatest impact George Washington had on the world was his Christian character. Washington was held in such high esteem by even his enemies that the mere mention of his name in association with a plan or a treaty or a piece of legislation would muster the needed support.

As a young man growing up in the wilderness, Washington gleaned the full advantage of the classical education of his father and older brother, though he was unable to study abroad. His rearing was replete with character training which prepared him for his divinely ordained position as first servant-leader of this nation.

The fact that Washington stands so tall among the other trees in America's forest is largely attributed to his humility, selflessness and quiet wisdom. Each of these traits issued from his intense love and appreciation of the Heavenly Father and His Son. Washington was a devout believer in Christ in the truest sense.

His instructions to the nation contained abundant admonishments to follow the paths of righteousness in domestic and foreign affairs alike. America has yet to experience his equal in the demonstration of the ideals of Christian leadership.

Noah Webster (1758-1843)

Noah Webster has been called the "Schoolmaster of the Nation" and the "Father of American Scholarship and Education." Born and raised in Connecticut, Webster attended Yale as a youth, taking time off to serve in the Continental Army during the War for Independence. Webster was indefatigable in his efforts to secure a place of stature for young America in the family of nations. It was Noah Webster who prevailed upon Washington and others to discard the weak and vulnerable Articles of Confederation in preference to a stronger and more stable federal constitution.

Webster's biblical understanding of government enabled him to speak to the nation in a manner which solidified the mold of philosophical and political thought for many generations. As a young man, Webster held to the basic tenets of Christianity and saw life from a biblical worldview. It was not, however, until he reached a half-century in age that he came to a saving knowledge of Jesus Christ.

This experience served to heighten his mission to instruct the nation in biblical truth. His governmental catechisms and moral teachings were instrumental in educating the nation in the Christian principles of character and service. So widespread in use were his textbooks, including the famed "blue-backed speller" and his annotated translation of the Holy Scriptures, that Webster's renown and influence during the early years of the republic were second only to that of George Washington.

References

Verna M. Hall, *The Christian History of the American Revolution: Consider and Ponder* (San Francisco: Foundation for American Christian Education, 1976).

Julian Hawthorne, ed., *Orations of American Orators,* vol. I (New York: The Colonial Press, 1900).

Rosalie J. Slater, *Teaching and Learning America's Christian History: The Principle Approach* (San Francisco: Foundation for American Christian Education, 1965; 1993).

Noah Webster, *The American Dictionary of the English Language* (1828 facsimile edition, San Francisco: The Foundation for American Christian Education, 1967; 1995). See especially Preface: "Noah Webster: Founding Father of American Scholarship and Education" by Rosalie J. Slater.